Wells in Pictures

Then and Now

Roger Arguile

Copyright © Roger Arguile

This edition 2023 published by Jubilee Publications,
Wells-next-the-Sea, NR23 1EG

ISBN 978-0-9568515-2-9

Designed by Sara Phillips
Printed by Gomer Press, Llandysul, Ceredigion SA44 4JL

The photographs which make up this collection come from many sources. Many photographs have been reproduced so often that it is impossible to know where the copyright is held.

However, the heart of this book consists of those pictures taken by Richard Shackle of the Norfolk Library Service who took more than a thousand pictures between 1969 and 1979, most of them in 1970. Many others come from the Comma collection, a labour of love produced by the Local History Group some years ago. Others are from John Tuck's considerable collection of over 2000 photographs. Betty Tipler took hundreds of pictures between 1968 and 2006. Others come from photographs submitted to the Facebook group *Wells – Down Memory Lane*. We owe a good deal to those who took and those who collected and preserved pictures such as these. This collection owes everything to them. In order to complete the series there are photographs taken over the last two or three years showing the town as it is now. I am indebted to Linda Gower who took most of them. The information explaining the changes which the town has undergone comes from my own research and from that of Mike Welland over a long period of time. For his considerable assistance I am deeply grateful.

Finally, I have both amended and substantially added to the material published in the first edition. I hope that by extending its scope I have provided a pictorial history which supplements the stories I have told elsewhere, but inevitably, even as this comes to print, there will be further changes and will continue to be so. Life ever moves on.

Front cover: Wells-next-the-Sea, East Quay 2022 (author's photograph)
Top left: Model T Fords outside The Fleece in 1910 (McCallum)
Bottom left: The Fleece in 2020 (Gower)

Contents

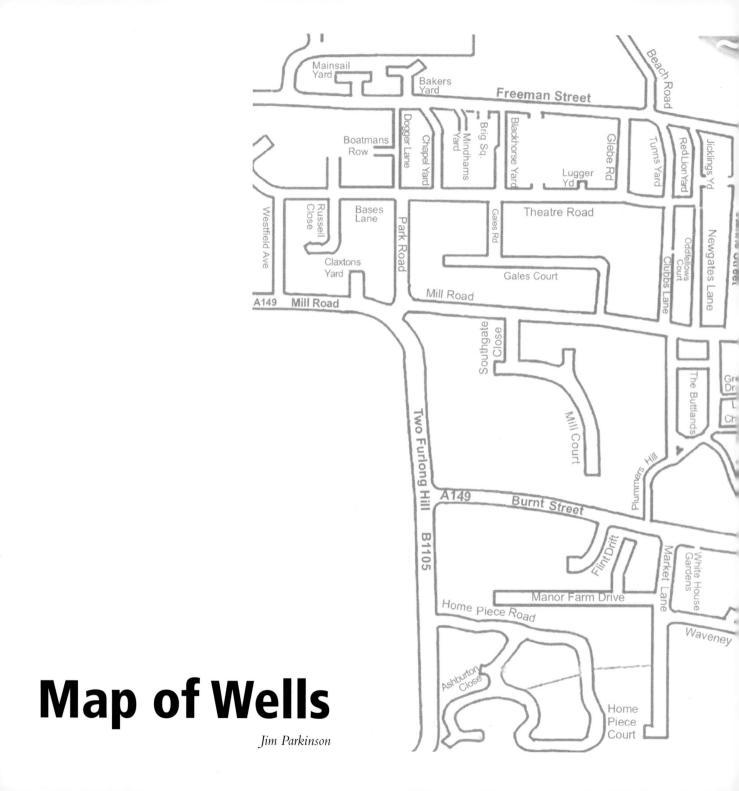

Map of Wells

Jim Parkinson

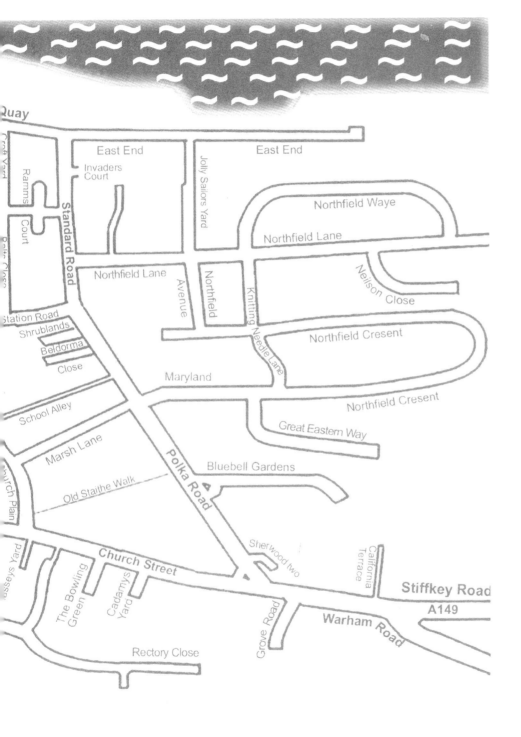

Introduction

Wells-next-the-Sea has become a much sought-after holiday resort, so much so that many of those who come for a holiday want to buy into the town so that they can stay whenever they want. But its character is in good part due to its having been for a long time a port, a fishery and an industrial town set in rich farmland.

The fishing has changed its character over centuries. Its major fishery is shellfish – crabs, lobsters and pre-eminently whelks. When the first written record of its fishing appeared in 1337 it had thirteen boats fishing by line or net for anything there was: herring, cod and their allies, rays, even eels. Fish migrate as they wish and competing fishing boats – from different countries – must follow them as they can. Thus in the fifteenth century there grew up the vast industry of cod fishing, first in the middle of the North Sea and thence to Iceland. The decline of both herring and cod fishing had, in those days, little to do with scarcity, more to the mysterious movements of fish but most of all to governments and wars.

The same boats that went for fish might make a living by trade. By the sixteenth century vessels from Wells were routinely bringing coal from the north-east of England and taking grain, barley, wheat and malt, to provide for the miners of those same ports and their populations at large. The trade was regular and important. It accounts for the number of merchants' houses in the town, as the many yards which run down to the quay housed mariners, fishermen, maltsters, shipbuilders, agricultural labourers and their families.

Wells has also always been a country town as Norfolk was an agricultural county. The happy combination of sheep farming and barley growing – the sheep fertilised the thin soil as well as providing cheese, fleece and meat – led both to the growth of the Norfolk wool industry as well as the trade in malt. So successful was it that by the eighteenth century, a third of the exports of malt to the continent passed through Wells customs. By the nineteenth century malting had become commercialised and industrialised, based on the town itself.

The signs of the town's past are less visible than they once were; a number have disappeared over the last fifty years. Even until the 1990s there was evidence of the commercial and industrial character of the town, as a port, as a manufactory of malt and a processor of animal feed.

The pages that follow are intended to give some visual clues as to what it looked like in times not so long past and how it came to be as it is.

The Port

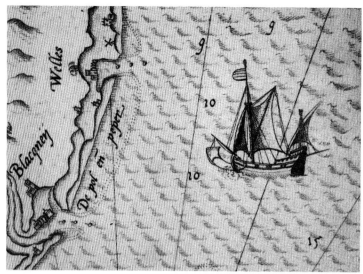

Lucas Waghenaer's 16th century chart showing Wells and Blakeney (north is to the right)

Sailing vessels lining the quay in 1880 – brigs, schooners, ketches and a steam tug, *Promise*, in the 1880s (Tuck)

A steamer is taken out to sea by the steam tug *Marie*, while a sailing vessel sits against the quay in 1901 (Tuck)

Bottom right:
Waggons hauled by horses along the quay (Tuck)

The importance of the harbour to overseas vessels as well as those along the coast is evidenced by its appearance on charts. That of the famous Dutch cartographer, Lucas Waghenaer in 1586 shows it to be, along with Blakeney, an important port. The trade with the continent became significant so that by 1750 it was the second biggest exporter of malt to the continent carrying a third of the trade to Holland.

By the nineteenth century Wells was not only the home of several dozen colliers and fishing vessels; it also built them in numbers. While most were up to 120 tons it occasionally built larger vessels over 300 tons. All were sailing vessels carrying three and occasionally four masts; Wells never went over to building steel vessels or those powered by steam.

Steam powered vessels began to make their appearance by the turn of the twentieth century. Initially, they were too expensive. Wind was free and the space taken up by bunkering coal reduced the space for cargo and hence profitability. The larger the ship the less of a problem this would be. One use of steam was the provision of a steam tug to tow vessels in and out of the harbour, which was often difficult to achieve in the case of sailing vessels. This saved time and money and made entry to the harbour much safer. *Marie* was the last of

The quay in 1939 (Britton)

Vic 55 was still entering the harbour as late as 1979 (Comma)

four such vessels, the first being *Economy* in 1840. (*Marie* was requisitioned by the government in 1915 and sunk by hitting a mine shortly thereafter.)

The coming of the railway in 1857 was supposed to enhance the viability of the port. A tramway from the station was built to enable cargoes to be shipped from the holds of vessels onto waggons. Hauled by horses, these would be taken to the end of the quay for onward shipment to London and the south or to the breweries of the Midlands. But in fact, while vessels could be stormbound, the railways could carry cargo faster and in any weather.

Spritsail barge *Alf Everard*

Piles of beet on the quay in November 1933
(*The Times*)

Loading in the 1950s carrying sacks on
barrows (Tuck)

The gradual replacement of sailing vessels by steamers may have slowed the decline but did not prevent it. The second world war brought an end to all coastal traffic, other than a few vessels bringing in cement for the airfield runways. Motor vessels were becoming common but whereas oil had to be imported, coal was in abundance. The last steamer to enter Wells harbour was *Vic 55*, built during the war for just that reason. Her last trip to Wells was in 1979.

Post-war, among the last of the sailing ships to trade with Wells were the spritsail barges belonging to the Everards company of Greenhithe. Each was named after a member of the family. *Alf Everard* and *Ethel Everard* were regular visitors to the harbour.

The very last commercial sailing vessel to enter the harbour was *Albatros*, a Dutch barge which continued to bring soya into the port as late as 1996 and which was, for some years, moored against the quay trading as a pub and restaurant.

Between the wars various attempts had been made to revive the harbour. In 1933 the British Sugar Corporation agreed to take sugar beet from local farms by sea to Selby on the Humber. The *Times* newspaper hailed it with the headline 'Return to Prosperity' after the shock of the closure of the maltings.

For a couple of years in the autumn months sugar beet lay on the quay in huge piles. Some was loaded direct from the farms down chutes. But the trade came abruptly to an end in 1935 despite attempts by the Urban District Council to get it to continue. Beet remained a major crop but it would be taken over land to the processing plants in Peterborough and King's Lynn.

After the war, trade remained slow.

The scene from the Granary in 2021 (Arguile)

Methods of loading and unloading relied upon muscle power. Grain was brought in sacks from local farms to be taken by barrow along a narrow plank to be emptied into the hold.

A major revival post-war was brought about by the use of artificial fertilisers and animal feed. It was remarkable in its scale and suddenness. In 1964 there were thirty-four inward movements; by 1967 seventy-three vessels came into the harbour. By in 1982 there were 258 inward movements.

It brought employment to the town. Men were employed in loading and unloading vessels; some took to joining the crew, some just for one trip, some for several. Bulk cargoes were often unloaded with shovels; the holds had to be fully emptied and swept before another cargo could be loaded. Such were the numbers of vessels that on some spring tides there would be as many as eight vessels double-banked in the harbour.

Right top: *MV Nederland* in September 1964 with 380 tons of Kainit fertiliser in paper sacks. It would take out 400 tons of barley (Press picture)

Right bottom: Eight vessels double-banked in the 1960s (EDP)

Top: *Ni-Tricia* towing a coaster into the quay, stern first (Alec Tuck)

Centre: *Vixen*, *Tramp* and another vessel aground waiting for the tide (Tipler)

Bottom: *Klaas I* awaiting the tide some time in 1987 (Seeley)

Ships could only be unloaded while against the quay wall, so vessels might have to tie up alongside another vessel to await the unloading of the nearer vessel which might then have to be loaded with a fresh cargo. Latterly most vessels left in ballast, in other words, empty, their ballast tanks filled with sea-water. Soya became the major import, to be used as animal feed on the nearby farms.

When a boat arrived offshore its skipper would radio the pilot. Generations of pilots guided vessels into the port, climbing on board from the pilot boat. Latterly it was the *Ni-Tricia* that guided vessels in, sometimes turning a vessel round in the narrow channel by pushing with its bow. It was a curious craft, a steel boat built in a Chesterfield back garden by its owner, Nigel Hingley.

Pilotage was necessary: the narrow channel, which was constantly changing, required local knowledge. Sometimes, vessels trying to get in on an earlier tide would find themselves aground and having to wait until the next tide. Occasionally skippers would understate the

Unloading by grab with tarpaulin wind shield, 1980s (Barker)

Loading *Subro Valour* with peas; harbourmaster 'Chick' Smith on extreme right (Whitaker)

Captain Francis Moeller, pilot 'Boy' Court, Bob Newstead, shipping agent Brian Barker and mayor Myrtle French (Barker)

draught of their vessel in an attempt get in on an earlier tide. They might end up sitting on the sand having to wait for the next flood tide. Grounding could cause damage, for instance to the rudder, which on occasion might have to be welded up between tides, much cheaper than a dry dock. Local skills were usefully employed.

The harbour was busy throughout the year though most especially in the autumn when fertiliser was required. Vessels came from Holland, from Germany, both west and east, from Scandinavia and from Denmark but also occasionally from along the British coast. Regular visitors were those of the Sully brothers, all named 'Subro' to which was added an identifier beginning with V: thus *Subro Valour*, *Subro Viking* and so on. The Everards vessels following a similar pattern, giving the vessels names ending in 'ity' as in *Agility*.

Methods of loading had improved. The grab on the end of a mobile crane was a favoured method though it made for a lot of dust which was not appreciated by some residents. A tarpaulin attached to vertical girders alleviated the problem to some degree. Elevators could be used for loading. Another method was the use of a suction hose which hung from the gantry of the granary run by Favor Parker of Stoke Ferry. It caused less dust but could often become clogged.

Some vessels became old friends. The *Tramp*, registered at Thyborøn in Denmark, was a regular visitor. Its fiftieth trip was marked by a presentation. It eventually made over eighty trips into the harbour. Its captain, Francis Moeller, married a local girl, Elizabeth Cox.

Tramp was later lost at sea though no lives were lost. Moeller would bring his

Double-banked vessels in the 1980s, and a full car park (Tuck)

The *Albatros* in her days as a quayside pub and restaurant 2018

The quay now with fishing boats and heavily used as a car park 2022 (Arguile)

new boat *Othonia* into the harbour just to visit the place.

The end of the trade came suddenly. Vessels were getting larger; the harbour was silting up. Favor Parker withdrew from the town; regulations became tighter and farmers' needs had changed. The end came in 1992 when the last motor vessel entered the harbour. The Dutch sailing barge *Albatros* soldiered on for a few years before being converted into a quayside restaurant. Sold by its skipper, Ton Brouwer, it was sent away for extensive repairs – it was built in 1899 – returning to Wells in 2023.

Now it would be mostly fishing vessels that would line the harbour wall together with a wind farm supply vessel. Pontoons for the use of visiting leisure boats were added. The outer harbour, built in 2009 for wind farm support vessels, would be made available for the same purpose.

The Quay

At the turn of the twentieth century, as the port declined, so malting seemed to boom. It was at this time, in 1904, that the Granary was built. Just as the port declined so the quayside changed. The scaffolding poles can be seen behind the railway trucks in the picture below.

The Granary and its environments, so iconic and so dominant, merit more than a second glance.

Built by F&G Smith in 1904, the Granary was intended to store and facilitate the export of barley and malt both overseas and coastwise. After the closure of their various maltings in 1929, Vynne & Everett, grain merchants of Swaffham, rented the building with an option to purchase.

In 1961, they sold out to Favor Parker,

The quay in 1904 (Tuck)

The quay in the 1920s with adjacent maltings (Tuck)

The quay in 1992 (Tipler)

The quay with the granary converted into flats in 1996 (Gower)

feed merchants of Stoke Ferry, who set about importing animal feed and fertiliser all of it from overseas which generated the coaster trade that boomed in the 1970s and 80s, as seen previously.

Once the coasters had gone, Favor Parker having relocated all their operations to Stoke Ferry, the decision had to be made as to what to do with the Granary. Its demolition was proposed, but its conversion into flats made financial sense, although it required huge amounts of internal works and the piercing of the frontal with windows. The several recesses provided space for small balconies, thus giving the unique selling point of the finest views out to sea over the marshes, reminiscent of the high windows of merchants' houses two centuries before. At the time the Granary was built, the quayside consisted almost entirely of industrial buildings, including several maltings and several public houses. These disappeared, one by one.

On the quay itself a number of buildings, including several butchers, had survived the rebuilding of the quay area in the 1840s. They had been taken over by TC Grange's haulage business, carrying foodstuffs to and from the quay. It was probably when the post-war government nationalised motor transport that these properties were no longer needed. They were removed in the 1950s.

The south side of the quay was to go through several piecemeal changes reflecting changing uses. Its industrial nature would gradually be lost. The closure of the maltings in 1929, described in detail on pages 26-27 onwards, was but the first stage. Some buildings were refaced with their changed use; others were demolished. Perversely, this piecemeal approach over many years was to preserve a lot of the character of the

Above: The Lord Nelson and the Golden Fleece between industrial buildings (Tuck)

Above right: An amusement arcade and petrol pumps in the 1960s (Tuck)

The Lord Nelson's premises remain but its use changed (Tuck)

Rebuilding after the fire in 2005 – with more to come (Gower)

town which is now so beloved of tourists. The tourism potential was recognised early after the Second World War with the opening of the Pinewoods campsite at the end of the Beach Road, followed by the provision of entertainment and refreshment on the quay.

By the 1960s most of the buildings, including the pubs and shops, had been knocked down and replaced by tourist attractions including an amusement arcade. Sam Abel's garage with its tell-tale petrol pumps remained.

A fire in 2005 left the arcade empty for some years. It was demolished and replaced by a block of flats in imitation of the granary, with shops on the ground floor. Further development is expected.

The quay front either side of Staithe Street between the wars (Tuck)

Change happened progressively. The dour forbidding aspect of the quay's industrial buildings, relieved only by Sepping's two storey bay windows and his butchers' shop, one of seven pre-war, was to be altered first by the re-use of old buildings. Sam Abel's garage (see previous page) was established after the war. He had returned from the forces with an eye to buying up any property, and there were a few, available at sometimes knockdown prices. He was not alone in doing so – Charles Platten did something similar. The wholesale re-modelling of the east corner of Staithe Street in the 1970s partially achieved an improvement to the access to the street. The Golden Fleece to the west of Staithe Street alone survived unchanged in its exterior. It is the last of several pubs along the quay and to the east and west. It can be seen later on page 82.

Another example of the change was the fate of the former malting bought by the grain and coal merchants Vynne

The upper bay window remains but all below is changed (Tipler)

A completely new corner to Staithe Street in 2021 (Gower)

Vynne & Everitt's former malting, pre-1914 (Tuck)

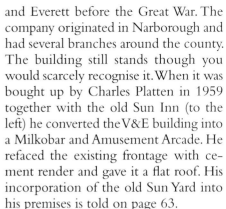

and Everett before the Great War. The company originated in Narborough and had several branches around the county. The building still stands though you would scarcely recognise it. When it was bought up by Charles Platten in 1959 together with the old Sun Inn (to the left) he converted the V&E building into a Milkobar and Amusement Arcade. He refaced the existing frontage with cement render and gave it a flat roof. His incorporation of the old Sun Yard into his premises is told on page 63.

French's fish shop to the right has not changed much but the huge garage belonging post-war to Grange's hauliers in 1959 became Stymans' delicatessen. Stymans' had long had a shop in Freeman Street but their move to the quay was not long lived. A series of retail outlets followed, the latest being a delicatessen. Again, the original structure remains but its plate glass windows replaced the huge doorways. Beyond it a hipped roof building, for many years Kay's Burger bar, replaced the earlier building while the frontage of Paul's malting remained virtually unaltered. It was all that remained of the huge No. 18 malting that ran all the way up Tunns Yard (see page 30).

Flat roof and shop front to the old maltings in 2021 (Gower)

Below left: Grange's garage in 1959 before conversion (French)

Below right: After conversion, Styman's the grocer in the 1960s (Tipler)

Fishing

Fishing in Wells has left few buildings of any permanence, mostly the sheds at the east end. What it has left are some of the old fishing boats, a few of which remain along the coast.

Wells was a fishing port from the early fourteenth century and probably long before. By the fifteenth century its men were bringing back salted and dried cod from Iceland. The cost in human lives is recorded in the town's burial register. The herring bonanza came and went and the herring fishery was latterly dominated by the Dutch. Oysters were dredged in the nineteenth century.

It was the whelk fishing which came

Whelkers by Tugboat Yard at the turn of the 20th century (Tuck)

to dominate in the twentieth century. Initially the pots were cast over the side one at a time, but eventually they attached to each other in shanks of eighteen or more with an anchor at each end and a Dan buoy on the surface so that they could be hauled up one-by-one.

If the rope was made of vegetable matter it would easily rot in sea water so both pots and rope would be coated in tar. A pot of tar gently boiling in the whelk sheds was a normal feature. Hand hauling was hard on the hands and may have been the cause of the large numbers of cases of septic hands, treated by the hospital in the 1930s.

It was for that reason that haulers driven by petrol engines, often taken from cars, were introduced. They con-

Jack, Billy and Jimmy Cox mending whelk pots (Tuck)

Alan Cox dropping
re-baited pots into the sea
(Comma)

'Gully', Reggie and Roly
Grimes at sea sieving
whelks (Tuck)

tinued in use until the 1980s. Eventually, hydraulic hauling would take the strain though pots had still to be lifted onto a steel table to be emptied, re-baited and stacked ready to be dropped back into the sea. Undersized whelks would be dropped back over the side together with the odd hermit crab while the much hated starfish would be left on the deck floor to dry out and die.

Fishing was mostly a family business – Coxes, Grimes, Jarvises, Peggs, Coopers, many of whom had come from along the coast in the early part of the century. Pots, once made of hazel, were weighed down with iron bases, called music because they resembled musical staves. They were later made with iron frames, supplied by local foundries and blacksmiths and bound with tarred rope. Their manufacture and repair was a routine occupation for fishermen when on shore. Modern whelk pots are square, made of plastic and are weighed down with concrete. The sea is hard on pots and crab and lobster pots still require constant attention if they are to prevent their inmates from escaping. Their repair remains an onshore task.

The whelks would be sieved and bagged at sea to be brought ashore and cooked in large boilers in the whelk sheds at the east end of the town. Not much had changed over more than fifty years.

'Loady' Cox with a basket of whelks (Tuck)

Stanley Frary boiling whelks (McNab-Grieve)

Whelks in boxes ready to be taken to the factory in King's Lynn (Arguile)

Whelks were taken to sheds at the east end of the quay to be cooked. Large coal-fired coppers were filled with water and heated in advance of the arrival of the fishing boats. A crew member would be sent on ahead to warn of their impending arrival. The bagged whelks were unloaded onto hand trucks, subsequently motorised, to be taken to the sheds. At one time (see page 18), they had been manhandled on yokes. With the disappearance of the coasters they could be unloaded onto the quay itself. After cooking, some would be taken to Grick's factory on Church Street to be removed from their shells then to be sold locally or taken to Billingsgate market in London. The rest were sold in their shells locally or elsewhere in the country. Wells was known nationally as the prime source of whelks. Over time however their popularity as a food began to decline and overseas markets, Korea in particular, were identified.

This local onshore industry was to be brought to an end by European regulations which judged the process unhygienic. In future the whelks would have to be taken to a facility in King's Lynn, being loaded straight from the boats in plastic boxes stacked five or six high onto a flatbed lorry. The whelk sheds would be used instead for boat storage, as artists' studios or for vivaria for the growing lobster fishery. Cox's shed was demolished to make way for a workshop for the harbour commissioners.

The boats themselves had scarcely changed in decades. Built of wood, until the 1920s they were powered by a single lug sail and oars, so that if the wind died, the crew might have to row ashore, beach the boat, walk home and go back to reclaim the boat on the next tide. Even after engines were fitted, sails

Right: Liverpool class ex-lifeboat *Spero II* being unloaded (Comma)

Below: *Romulus* and *Remus*, two of the Faversham trawlers

Bottom: *Blucher*, a GRP boat made from a mould of the *William Edward*

continued to be used; wind was free whereas petrol was expensive. The last wooden boat to be built for local fishermen was *Harvester* in 1951, built by the Emery brothers of Sheringham.

The next step was the use of retired Liverpool-class lifeboats such as the *Ann Isabella* and the *Spero II*. They were still built of wood but they were stronger and were equipped with more powerful engines. They lasted fifteen or more years before the next stage of development: larger boats made of different materials.

Boats with a different catch in view were the several trawlers coming from Kent in search of sprats and rays. Though no bigger than the whelk boats they were enclosed and operated in pairs sailing side by side. With a trawl net strung between them they brought in huge numbers of the small fish, sprats, which were then sent to Grimsby to be made into fish meal. The system had gained Alf Leggett, one of the new arrivals, an MBE for its invention long before he came to Wells. The five vessels, *Romulus*, *Remus*, *Cortina*, *Faustulus* and *Leona II*, came to visit and several remained to stay even after the sprats disappeared.

The trawlers were built of wood, as were the whelkers, though they were decked and had a wheelhouse. But wooden boats would become a rarity. The transition was marked by the *William Edward* being used as a plug, or mould, for the GRP boat, *Blucher*.

New materials enabled new designs. John Nudds was the first local fisherman to buy a GRP boat of new design, the *Isabelle Kathleen*. Previous boats had been double-ended to enable them to cope with following waves. The new boats were flat-sterned but were powerful enough to hold their courses. Many dif-

Top: *William Edward*, built in 1949, in full sail (Comma)

John Nudds and the *Isabelle Kathleen*

ferent hull shapes were tried, designed to improve speeds and layouts to facilitate the hauling, emptying and baiting process. The most radical was that of building boats with twin hulls whose stability and deck capacity were greatly increased. The first of such designs, *Pathfinder*, was succeeded by the *Two Brothers* in 2008 and then the very much larger *Nell Diana* in 2020 (see page 24). Most recently she has been joined by another twin-hulled vessel, the *Maggie Ann*.

Whelking was not the only fishery. In fact, over time, crabs and lobsters had become much more important, certainly in supplying the growing restaurant trade, but also processed locally for sale elsewhere in the country. A different kind of pot was required to catch them, a so-called parlour pot, rectangular in base with two entrances and the means of preventing the animals from escaping. As with whelk pots they were once made of hazel on an iron base with netting locally made but now usually bought in from elsewhere. Their necessary repair remains a local skill.

A new generation of fishing boats: the *Nell Diana* which arrived in 2020 (Arguile)

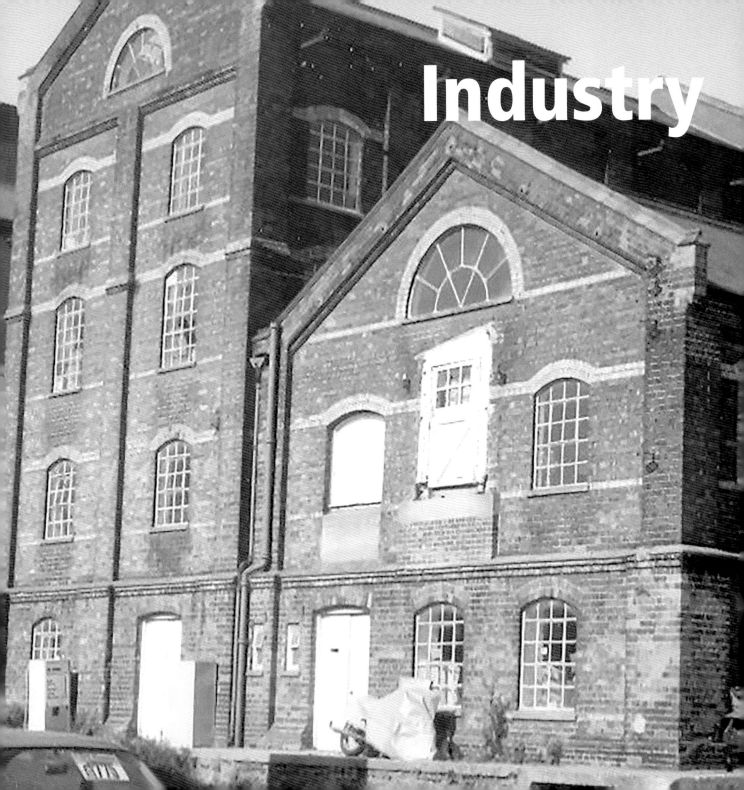

Industry

Above: These six composite pictures, from photographs taken in the 1970s, show the extent of the Eastern Counties Farmers' Co-operative estate. The yard is shown in the last picture where it fronts onto Staithe Street (Shackle)

Staithe Street maltings in 1970 (Shackle)

Wells was, until the latter part of the twentieth century, an industrial town. It was, during the early part of that period, also a major manufacturing town. Its major product was malt. Malt is made from barley, artificially made to germinate on huge malting floors to turn the starch in the grain into sugars. The germination process would be halted by kiln drying, the malted grain being ground up and boiled in water to dissolve the sugars and then, with the addition of yeast, allowed to ferment to produce alcohol.

There have been maltings in the town from the sixteenth century at least, when most were based on farms. Commercial malting in the nineteenth century resulted from the wider use of hops which act as a preservative as well as adding to the flavour of the beer; this enabled its transport over greater distances. Gradually the many maltings in the town were bought up by merchants rather than maltsters so that from the late 1870s onward they came into the hands of F&G Smith of Great Ryburgh. Smiths had plants in Dereham and Great Ryburgh but made their headquarters in Wells.

As consumption began to fall after the Great War and production methods became more efficient – and people had begun to drink less – there came the need to rationalise the business and it was de-

cided that it was the Wells estate which was to close. That happened literally overnight. In 1929 after hundreds of years of malting Wells was left with a dozen or so great maltings and grain stores left empty and gaunt to be cannibalised and allowed to decay.

Some of the buildings found other uses as grain stores and for other agriculturally-related purposes. Vynne and Everett, as already described, rented and then purchased the famous Granary on the quay. The largest complex of buildings was taken over by the Eastern Counties Farmers' Cooperative whose headquarters were in Ipswich in 1941. Pauls, maltsters also from Ipswich, came the same year. Favor Parkers came in 1961. All have gone.

Eastern Counties Farmers' Cooperative first established a presence in Wells in 1935 on Staithe Street, expanding when their Yarmouth plant was bombed during the war. Their base was in Ipswich. Their several businesses were in the provision of seed, selling grain and other produce on behalf of their members – farmers in the district – manufacturing animal feed and selling farm machinery which they did from their facility in Fakenham. Their aim was to provide a comprehensive service to their members by buying and selling in bulk so as to obtain advantageous

Middle: The Sun Yard malting in 1975 (Shackle)

Bottom: Malthouse Place which replaced it, taken in 2020 (Gower)

The tallest building in Wells, seen from the beach bank circa 1900 (Tuck)

No 3 malting on Star Yard, off Staithe Street, in 1970 (Shackle)

Star Yard in 2020 (Gower)

prices and to deal with processors on their behalf. They supplied farms with animal feed they mixed themselves.

Wells was at the furthest end of their activities and their proposals to modernise the plant were never fulfilled. They pulled out in 1971. The composite picture on the previous page shows a panoramic view taken from Staithe Street of the ECFC plant, going clockwise from the south showing the large malting adjacent to Sun Yard, and offices. The present malting lies behind the northern end seen in the penultimate picture.

The larger malting on the ECFC site lay derelict for several years. With its kiln roof it had once stood so high that together with the Paul's malting on Tunns Yard, it dominated the skyline from seawards.

Despite attempts to save it, it was demolished in 1979 and was replaced by a block of flats to be called Malthouse Place and designed with features intended to give some indication of the land's former use (see previous page).

Standing in Staithe Street by the Wells maltings but looking east is Star Yard. (which used to lead to Stoughtons Yard, running down to the quay). In Star Yard was another malting. The hoist used for lifting the sacks of barley to the upper floors can be seen projected from the building. Again it is quite gone, and the yard now gives access only to storerooms belonging to the nearby hardware store.

That the Staithe Street malting survived was due in part to central government changing its mind about Norfolk's housing requirements. There was also the resistance of the newly formed Wells Community Association and a recently formed arts group called the Wells Centre. Many of the other buildings were demolished as we have already seen. After nine years

Wells maltings 2023
(Gower)

Michael Hooton, John
Plumbe, Ronald Stennett
Willson and Jonathan
Field outside the
Sackhouse

of fundraising the Association obtained the lease, cleared the building of rubble, pigeon droppings and rusting machinery and created a community space and a little theatre within the building.

The other building that survived was the Sackhouse which runs down Jicklings Yard (see page 63). It had become the base for the Wells Centre which had leased it from Wells UDC a year or so before. Coming from the arts world, its promoters were led by local glass designer Ronald Stennett Wilson. The Sackhouse itself became a coffee bar and art gallery but the wider purpose of the Centre was to put on plays and high-end musical events in the larger building, very different from the broader local interests of the Community Association. Over the years it would obtain the services of world-famous musicians through artistic contracts but local support was patchy and it closed in 1991. Thereafter its theatrical role was taken over by the Granary Players under the aegis of the newly formed Friends of the Granary.

The condition of the outer shell gave cause for concern and in 2016 a huge fundraising project was launched to refurbish the whole building and to create a larger arts complex and community space paid for with money from the National Lottery. The Sackhouse would be part of the refurbishment.

The second most prominent malting in the town was also the last to cease working. Part of it can still be seen standing on the quay. Sometimes known as Pauls' malting it came to be so called because, after the closure of all the Wells maltings, having lain empty for ten years it was bought by Pauls of Ipswich in 1941 after one of its works in that town had been requisitioned by the government for the war effort. It was a huge enterprise,

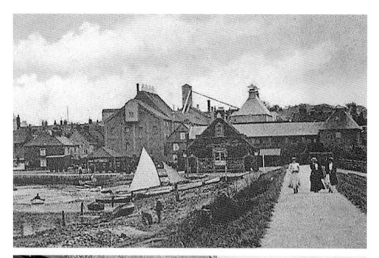
No 18 Pauls' malting in the 1900s (Tuck)

Malting No 18 seen from Red Lion Yard (Shackle)

Modern houses replaced the malting shown above in 1980 (Gower)

running all the way up the hill almost as far as Theatre Road from the quay.

It was part of a huge complex: its various malting floors being supplied from a tower, seen left, whose chutes delivered barley from a central grain store. Grain was first delivered to a steeping chamber where barley was soaked to promote germination before being shovelled onto one of its two malting floors. The process was continuous. Temperature control was achieved by opening and closing the louvres (see picture centre left) on each floor. The malting barley was turned each day for a fortnight with a wooden malt shovel, during which time it would germinate, turning its starch into sugars. Finally, there was the kiln into which the malt was barrowed in order the stop the germination and roast it.

After Pauls withdrew in 1961 the building again lay empty. The firm of Rileys took on the task of demolishing the huge three floored malting in the 1980s to replace it with a row of town houses.

To the east of Staithe Street running parallel to it is Bolts Close (running down to Croft Yard). On its west side stood another huge malting at its junction with

Shop Lane looking west to a former malting (Shackle)

Shop Lane from the same aspect in 2020 (Gower)

Shop Lane. In the picture (top left) we can see the grain store. The whole complex stretched down Croft Yard, beginning with the steeping chamber where the barley was soaked, to the 'store' where malting took place, to the kiln where germination was stopped.

The plan below of an auction of other properties including the manager's house (see page 78) in 1903 and demarcated with the heavy lines, shows the illustrated buildings, No 1 Malt Store above. This part of the town was dominated by malt related buildings.

There are several survivors of the carnage to be seen by the perceiving eye. Almost by a miracle, on the opposite side of Croft Yard, the oldest identifiable malting in the town still remains. Bought by Thomas Bunting in 1584, it passed through many hands before being acquired by Smiths. In 1970 it looked very forlorn. However, having been turned

The same building as above from the south (Shackle)

The view as left in 2020 (Gower)

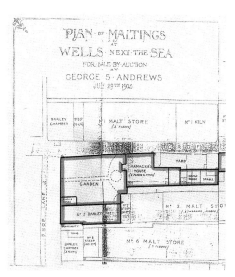

Sixteenth century malting on the east side of Croft Yard in 1979 (Shackle)

Buntings maltings in 2020 (Arguile)

into some fine town houses it looks now as if it might see out its half millennium.

There are other survivors. The Pop Inn at the south end of the Beach Road had a more serious purpose both as a malting and then, under the ownership of Vynne and Everett, as a grain store. Intent upon preserving the character of the area, its extension to the north, on the site of the old coal vault, is of a similar style. For some time, part of it was given over to a children's indoor playground. There are now proposals to turn it into a street food restaurant.

Beach Road maltings in
1970 (Shackle)

Beach Road maltings in
1970 (Shackle)

Beach Road maltings in
2020 (Gower)

The Glebe marked the western end of the maltings. Along its eastern side were some of the smaller and probably older malting buildings which were taken over for various uses after the 1929 closure. Tom Grange, local haulier, had some of his garages there, south of which, up the hill, was the Marina Amusement Arcade, also now gone. It had dodgem cars in it. In the 1970s all were demolished and a row of houses built using reclaimed bricks from the maltings.

The picture on page 35 of the top of the Glebe in 1970 shows the tower from which barley was distributed to the various maltings with the ruins of the foundry in the foreground.

Iron foundries in both Wells and Wals–

Top left: The Glebe with former maltings buildings re-used by TW Grange for his haulage business

Top right: The Glebe in 2020 with town houses(Gower)

Bottom left: Grange's garage which occupied part of the site in 1970 (Shackle)

Bottom right: The same buildings looking north in 1970 (Shackle)

ingham had long supplied items for the shipbuilding industry, agriculture and the maltings in addition to the several black-smiths. Patented iron kiln tiles used to dry and roast the finished malt were widely used locally. John Woods had been a blacksmith and ironfounder since the 1820s, first in Staithe Street and then as here on the Glebe. It was sold to Jabez Cornish in 1885 whose family business included a foundry at Walsingham and one in Fakenham. He advertised himself as a wheelwright, manufacturing agricul-

tural items including hay elevators, threshing machines, ploughs, corn and seed drills as well as the kiln tiles used by the maltings. The business closed shortly after the maltings in 1932.

The recent picture (left) shows the removal of all traces of malting and the piercing of the end wall of Foundry House with windows. The old foundry buildings have gone.

Boroughs and Strattons ran a bulk feed carrying business from Shop Lane, previously a private yard belonging to Smiths. Smiths had been advised immediately pre-war to realise as many of their properties as they could to minimise losses reckoned likely as a result of the war, which effectively killed the coastal trade. Post-war the buildings were bought out

Boroughs & Strattons/
Dalgety's entrance on
Standard Road (Shackle)

by Dalgety's who subsequently moved to Egmere on the Fakenham Road four miles away. The name Stratton survives in the little close that runs north from it.

The close opposite is named Ramms Court after a local butcher who owned land around the town. This is an example of the infilling referred to by the council which it claimed never benefitted local people. Adjacent to it, No. 6 malting, whose pagoda-like cowls can be seen in the upper left picture in 1970, was taken down in 1988 as can be seen in the bottom picture, to be replaced once again by housing.

Stratton Place 2020
(Gower)

Malting was not the only industry in the town. The milling of wheat had been carried on for centuries and the naming of Mill Road is a clue to the fact that there were once half a dozen windmills on the crest of the ridge which runs parallel to the quay. The last to go, in 1903, was a smock mill on the brow of the hill on Northfield Lane. In its stead, in 1893, a huge modern mill was built close by the railway station on Maryland by Dewing & Kersley. The machinery was driven by a steam engine, which also provided electrical power to light the interior, hence the tall chimney. Its 'Sunshine Flour', most suitable for cakes and biscuits, was sold throughout the region and to Peek Freans in London and Jacobs in Liverpool.

Dismantling of No 6
malting in 1988 (Tipler)

Mains electricity caused the chimney to go first after the war. A huge grain silo was added in the 1960s intended to maximise storage capacity but which proved to be unsuitable and which put the company into difficulties. It closed in 1980. The silo, (opposite, bottom right) which survived when the mill was demolished in 1984 was itself taken down in 2022.

Dewing and Kersley's flour mill before about 1910 – note the steam lorry (Comma)

Bottom left: Smock mill on Northfield Lane, demolished in 1903 (Tuck)

Bottom centre: The offices and grain silo in 2020 (Gower)

Bottom right: The silo being demolished 2022 (Arguile)

The Railway

A windmill, a steam driven mill and the railway station, late 1800s (Tuck)

Taxis waiting to take visitors back to the station (Tuck)

East Quay with railway waggons (Tuck)

The railway came to Wells in 1857. It was intended to carry freight to and from the harbour, and agricultural produce to inland markets, thus bringing wealth to the town. The Earl of Leicester, a great agriculturalist was its major investor. Freight between the harbour and the station yard was carried by a tramway which ran from the station around the east side of the town to the harbour. Locomotives were not allowed on the quay and waggons were moved by horses (see page 2) and later by lorry. Opened in 1859 it was supposed to improve the harbour's fortunes. In fact, because the railway could carry freight in increasing quantities faster and because rail travel was not affected by storms at sea, the coming of the railway led to the decline of the port.

However, the railway brought tourists into the town. In the years between the wars day tourists came in numbers from inland so that a number of enterprising folk offered a taxi service from the station to the beach. A bus service was provided for the same purpose. Latterly pilgrims came to Walsingham by train and the carriages were stored at Wells during the day until they were needed for the return journey.

The station buildings included the entrance and booking hall, offices, the porticoed train shed and an engine shed with a turntable.

In 1866 a second line was built to the west taking traffic to Heacham and from there to King's Lynn. The line was never very successful but it was made less so because the Heacham platform was outside the train shed and transfer from the Heacham line to the Dereham/Norwich line was not straightforward.

So in 1935, the shed was demolished to make way for open platforms each

Above: The station as
originally built in 1857;
picture taken in 1909
(Tuck)

Right: Passenger train
heading towards
Heacham in 1952, the
year the line was closed

Far right: The station
booking hall with
platform canopy in 1956
(Comma)

Diesel railcars had better acceleration than steam (Tuck)

Wells station in 1956 (Tuck)

The same view of the old station yard in 2020 (Gower)

with its own canopy, making Wells a genuine junction. But the Heacham line was never profitable and closed to passenger traffic in 1952; and when the line was swept away in the 1953 floods no effort was made to restore it for goods traffic.

The railways were nationalised in 1948 and diesel railcars were introduced in 1955 producing a faster service carrying workers to Norwich and school pupils to Fakenham. It would be possible to leave Wells at 6.50am and arrive in Norwich by 8.30am in time to walk to one of the many factories and offices which still flourished in the city. Wells children who attended Fakenham Grammar School could catch the train there and back each day.

Following the Beeching Report of 1963 the line closed on October 3rd 1964. The vast estate of lines and sidings, replete with sheds and a turntable to turn steam engines around for the return journey were all to disappear within a short time. Two views from the same spot show how dramatically it has changed.

Demolition proceeded quite quickly. By 1965 the platform canopies had been removed, the lines lifted and the station buildings partially demolished. The train shed, the turntable, the sidings and the various lines into the station were removed leaving an area of ten acres which the council proceed to buy in 1967, intending it for industrial development. By 1970 only one company had tendered for a lease and subsequently withdrew. Subsequently English Industrial Estates, a government agency charged with developing sites for industry in rural areas had a number of units erected which were then taken up by Cartwright and Butler, who had a preserves

Top left: The tracks were removed, leaving the platforms, in 1966 (Tuck)

Top right: The platform canopies were removed (Tuck)

Middle left: The frontage and booking hall were partially demolished (Shackle)

Middle right: The harbour branch after removal of the tracks (Tipler)

Bottom: The station frontage in 1970 (Shackle)

manufactory on Mill Road. They knocked them into one. In 1968 the bridge over Two Furlong Hill was lifted. The tramway from the station to the quay had its rails partially lifted, though those running along the east quay remained; they were simply covered over with tarmac, where in odd places they can still be seen.

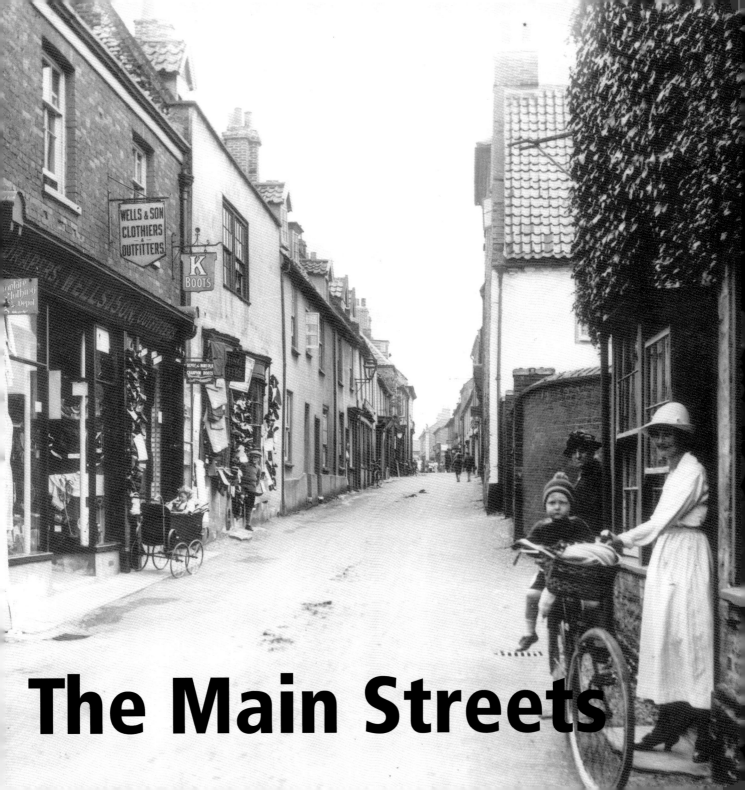

The Main Streets

Above: Looking north beyond the sweet shop is Wells outfitters, long gone (Comma)

Bottom left: The cottages on the right made way for ECF Yard (Comma)

Bottom right: Former Cadamy's electricians shop, now selling tourist items (Gower)

Staithe Street

The northern end of the town was dominated by maltings and other industrial buildings. There were however a large number of retail outlets selling most things to meet local needs from food to clothing, from hardware to horse furniture. Almost everything that a person could want was available in the town. In many cases there was a choice as to which of a number of shops one would patronise, even for clothing. When it came to food shops there were at one time seven butchers and four bakers. Grocers selling processed food were just becoming popular.

The number of businesses supplying food was to shrink in number and those selling clothes and footwear were almost to disappear. The several trades associated with horses disappeared from the town early in the century.

Staithe Street – the name means harbour – is now the main shopping street. It looks for all the world as if it has scarcely changed. The truth is that what was for sale has changed many times over the years and some of the buildings have been dramatically replaced. Thus, towards the bottom of the hill the shop fronts on the east side remain recognisable, but there is no longer an outfitters and the

Top left: After the gas explosion in 1911 (Comma)

Top right: International Stores in 1970 (Shackle)

Middle left: Leftley's expanded premises in 2023 (Gower)

Middle right: Butchers' Drapery on Staithe Street between the wars (Tuck)

Bottom: The same shop in 2021 (Arguile)

sweet shop long ago became an electricians, now also gone. On the other side the cottage to the right, which stood next to the still standing maltings, was replaced by the ECF Yard which became a car park and is now the new community centre as we saw on page 29. The house opposite is now a hardware shop.

At the other end of the street on the west side stands the very grand frontage of Leftley's grocers with its ionic columns. It has survived, little changed, since 1861 when Wells was a prosperous port, but it nearly didn't. After Thomas Leg-

gett, draper, outfitter and milliner had sold it to the International Tea Stores in 1911 there was a gas explosion which nearly wrecked it. It remained with International as a grocers' shop until 1985.

Another survivor is another former draper's, that of Herbert Butcher, which has even retained its wrought ironwork and the awning, now probably non-functioning, which would once have shaded customers who browsed its wares. It is now a gift shop and a café.

The upper east side of Staithe Street, has by contrast quite changed. Once it was the place of residence, known as Mayshiel, of Smiths the maltsters. The garden was behind a great wall and was fringed with ilex trees which ran a third of the way up the street to almost the southern corner. It is a reminder of the time when the street was dominated by large houses rather than shops, some of which would come to be built in front of the houses.

When Mayshiel was sold, its perimeter wall was demolished, the ilex trees taken down to be replaced by a parade of shops set back from the roadway, the last of which was built only in the last ten years.

At the bottom of the garden between Staithe Street and Bolts Close to the east, the new Health Centre was built in the 1970s, replacing the two doctors' surgeries, leaving a few token mature trees to give some indication of what had been there. The house itself which dates from the eighteenth century is described later (see pages 73-74).

The town once provided for all local clothing needs. We have already seen Herbert Butcher's shop. Wells and Co. men's and children's outfitters, tailors, hatters and drapers had several outlets on Staithe Street. One of the company's shops was where you could pay your

Top: Two of Wells and Sons' shops which flourished between the wars and afterward until the 1970s

Bottom: A convenience store and a former Cadamy's electrical shop in 2021 (Gower)

electricity bill. (The company ended up by taking on Butcher's outfitters' shop already mentioned.)

Another change is indicated by the presence of bollards intended to pedestrianise the street during the day. The road was too narrow to install pavements. Following pedestrianisation, visitors were able to browse the various outlets safely, which now sell lifestyle items rather than food or clothing. Small convenience stores have found it hard to compete with supermarkets and since the 2020 lockdown the pace of change has quickened. Several shops have simply closed.

Above: High Street in 1924 showing several of the twenty shops in the street (Tuck)

Below left: High Street in 2021 - some shop fronts still remain (Arguile)

Below right: Ramm's butchers shop, later Howells (Mahomet/Tuck)

High Street

High Street was at one time the main shopping street. Because it ran down to the church it was once known as Church Street. It boasted at one time three butchers, a baker, an ironmonger, a boot and shoe maker, several tailors and out-fitters, a greengrocer, a hairdresser and a musical instrument shop. It was until the 1840s the main thoroughfare out of town when Polka Road was built. A proposal in 1844 to knock down the houses on one side in order to widen the road was never implemented. Wells' first self service store was established in 1949 at the top of the hill. Changing hands it became a freezer shop before becoming a private house.

The shops had mostly gone by 1970. Howells the butchers, with its adjacent hat shop in the same ownership were the last to go. It is suggested that the closure of the railway in 1964 reduced the footfall in the street so that its shops became un-viable.

Of the many shops in the street, some have left no trace. Others have retained their shop fronts in order to preserve the look of the street if not its character. Eade's cycle dealer's shop (next page) was, before the war, also a hairdresser and to-bacconist. By 1970 it had become simply a hairdressers'. It is now a private house. At the southern end of the street was Thurgur's hardware shop which had been there for a hundred years. It closed in 1964, lying empty and increasingly der-elict for some time. The council thought of using it for its offices but in 1980 the whole block was knocked down to be replaced by six units extending into Marsh Lane. The demolition allowed the creation of a pavement by setting the houses back from the road. By the 1970s the town was not merely in decline but many of its buildings showed signs of

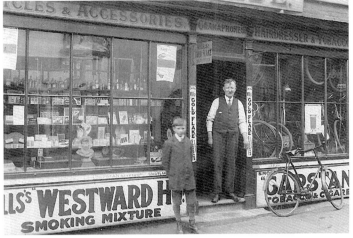

Top left: Eade's cycle shop in the 1930s (Tuck)

Top right: Eade's hairdressers in 1970 (Shackle)

Bottom left: Thurgur's shop at the corner of High Street and Church Plain (Tuck)

Bottom right: New houses on High Street, built in 1980 (Gower)

serious neglect. The opinion of Arnold Rogers, borough surveyor in the 1960s, was that the town needed to be modernised by wholesale slum clearance and the building of new houses. There was some demolition, as already shown. One or two were in a state of visible decay. Empty houses with broken windows were a not unusual feature of the street. A sign of the times, one or two were bought as holiday homes.

Some houses were demolished, and not replaced, notably at the bottom of the hill where number 64, a triangular building was taken down leaving a chimney

Right: 40 High Street in a state of decay in 1970 (Shackle)

Far right: 40 High Street in 2021 (Arguile)

Right: 64 High Street after demolition of the end house (Shackle)

Middle right: 64 High Street in 2022 (Ockwell)

Bottom right: Typical state of repair in 1970 (Shackle)

breast, a fireplace and the remains of a range. It remained as it was for some years before a door was put into the end wall, leaving the rest of the land as a parking place for cars.

Top: Church Plain in the
1900s, showing Thurgur's
shop and old houses to
the left, some of which
were demolished and
rebuilt in 1980 (Tuck)

Top right: Saab's sixteenth
century almshouses (Tuck)

Bottom left: Seen in the
early part of the 20th
century with the new
church hall

Bottom right: The church
hall in 1970 (Shackleton)

Church Plain

Another victim of the decline of shops
was the wide road in front of the church,
called Church Plain and once known as
'Jew town'. (No explanation has been
found.) Apart from the loss of Thurgur's
shop already mentioned it would lose
its baker's shop and its public house, the
Eight Ringers (see page 86). The former
stood adjacent to some of the oldest
houses in the town, the old almshouses
on its east side, built by William Saab,
merchant and churchwarden, in about
1599. Next door in 1891 would be built
Wells first police station.

The older houses opposite would
suffer equal change. Several of them
would be demolished in 1904 to make
way for the new church hall, for a while
a youth hostel. It can be seen in the picture to the left, set back from the road.
The houses had stables and haylofts
which would no longer be required, so
they were replaced in 1980. The loss of
the local residents means that however
well preserved the remaining houses are,
the street is empty and at night the
houses are dark. At weekends it is full of
cars.

Freeman Street looking west in the 1950s (Tuck)

Freeman Street

Freeman Street looking west 1960s with the Ship Inn in the foreground - parked cars where houses had been (Tuck)

Freeman Street in 2020, showing the Ship Inn building on the extreme left (Gower)

Freeman Street runs to the west of the town from the quay. The houses on the north side were built in the 1820s when it became a major shopping street named after its developer, John Freeman.

The most dramatic changes over the period have been at each end. The Ship Inn, seen centre left, gave up its licence in 1967, when it was transferred to the Ark Royal (see page 85), built on the site of several yards. The building is still there but the cottages to its west have gone, demolished in a wholesale operation in 1962. Initially intended for housing development all that was built there was the Ark Royal now also demolished. The pictures show the several stages of development. The bottom end of the car park can be seen at lower left.

As elsewhere the shops disappeared in the 1960s though a few remain. The grocers' shops in particular have gone, some to be replaced by restaurants and other food outlets.

Much of the 1820s developments on the north side of Freeman Street remain. On the south side one of the oldest extant houses in Wells, now called Merchant's House, stands at the corner of Blackhorse Yard. It appears on the 1793 census owned by one of the most significant families in the town, the Blooms. Now having no members in the town, they were a merchant family for long associated with the Normans (see page 75).

Elsewhere on the street a number of undistinguished houses in a poor state of repair were demolished and replaced by houses of similar size and character.

Something of the state of the old buildings and the yards that ran down to the street can be seen in the picture overleaf of the bottom of Theatre Yard, now completely gone. Grass grew in many places on those yards amidst conditions of life

Top left: 1820s development, north side (Shackle)

Top right: Merchant's House opposite in 1970 (Shackle)

Bottom left: Next to Brigg Square 1969 (Shackle)

Bottom right: The same plot in 2020 (Arguile)

Right: House, now demolished, at the bottom of Theatre Yard (Tuck)

which no one would now tolerate. It is now part of the Stearman's Yard car park.

Wells once boasted a number of corner shops; Freeman Street had several. The one on the corner of Mindhams Yard (overleaf) had a number of owners, one of whom was William Mindham, and was in its heyday a grocers and an out-fitters.

Mindham's grandson Frank Bell took over the business and ran it until his death in 1925 when it was taken over by the Styman brothers. They expanded in the town and in the 1950s moved out to a store which they converted from a garage

Frank Bell at his shop doorway before WWI (Welland)

Frank Bell at his shop doorway before WWI (Welland)

Bottom left: Styman Bros shop between the wars (Welland)

Bottom right: Former shop at the bottom of Mindhams Yard 2021 (Gower)

on the quay (see page 15).

Eventually the shop closed and was converted into flats. Corner shops were disappearing everywhere as larger stores belonging to chains which had greater buying power appeared. Shopping by car became the rule so that car parks were needed, something a small town with narrow streets could not provide.

It is at the far end of the street that the most dramatic changes have taken place. The houses on the north side ended with Auld's, subsequently Angus's bakery, beyond which was Barker's lorry garage. Barkers ran a haulage industry, carrying goods around the county and then long distance.

Top left: Auld's bakery in 1970 (Shackle)

Top right: Barker's garage pre-war (Barker)

Bottom left: Barker's garage and petrol station 1980s (Barker)

Bottom right: Bakers Yard and Mainsail Yard 2021 (Gower)

Subsequently they opened a repair garage which undertook vehicle testing. They sold up in 2000, allowing a development of three storey town houses preserving the memory of the bakery: one group of houses was named Bakers Yard. Another, fronting the street, ends with a four storey turreted building with excellent views of the marshes.

Flood risk was taken account of by the planners' insistence that the ground floor be given over to garages. Many of these have subsequently been turned into living accommodation. It is named Mainsail Yard, a reference to leisure sailing rather than the commercial sailing ships of long ago.

Top: Standard Road in the 1920s with a barn at the bottom of the road (Comma)

Bottom: Standard Road with the entrance to Shop Lane in 1970 (Shackle)

Right: Standard Road in 2020 (Gower)

Standard Road

Standard Road is the most easterly of the three major streets running down to the quay and is now a major thoroughfare connecting with Polka Road. The view of the marshes was once blocked by the Standard Barn. The left-hand turn onto the quay was difficult for vehicles to negotiate. Shop Lane, a private yard leading to the numbers 1, 2 and 6 of the maltings, later gave way to the Boroughs and Strattons premises which we saw on page 36. The white cottage on the bottom left picture was demolished in order to enable the widening and bending of the roadway and so as to allow the creation of a continuous pavement for pedestrians on the east side. A road once straight now had a kink it.

Cottage, now demolished, on Standard Road (Shackle)

The whelk factory behind the cottage above became a hardware shop (Gower)

Baker's cycle shop became Pope's garage, demolished in the 1990s and replaced by housing (Palfery)

The change wrought by demolition can be seen to greater effect when looking at the same buildings from the south east. The white cottage was demolished, the road widened and the east wall of what had previously been a whelk factory behind it was pierced by a number of windows and a doorway put in so that the whole could be made into a hardware shop. Part of the frontage was taken up by the widening of the road but the remainder provides an excellent display area for garden furniture and the storage of compost and aggregate for the business.

To the left of the shop can be seen another relic of Wells' past, Hayhoes barn. This was once one of a number of coal barns used for storage from the many colliers which since the sixteenth century and before had brought coal from the north east. For many years it was a the premises of James Case boat builder and now has become a private house.

Further up the road opposite Northfield Lane no trace remains of Baker's cycle shop which also sold petrol nor of Pope's garage which replaced it.

Polka Road

Originally named New Road, the road was built in 1845 as what would now be known as a by-pass to enable traffic to get to and from the quay easily. Waggons which had hitherto been forced to navigate up High Street where two waggons could not pass each other and whose surface was not metalled, could now proceed along a wide straight road down to the quay or to local maltings.

The young horse chestnuts, these days fully mature, can be seen as recently planted saplings in the picture at the lower left, taken in the early years of the century. The cottages uphill of the railway station can just be seen behind some trees. More visible is Dewing and Kersley's mill (see page 37). The mature trees on the right-hand side of the road have mostly gone and been replaced by several closes of housing.

Of the several garages were built in the 1920s in the town, two of them on Polka Road. They sprang up all over the town. Cars were unreliable and repairs constantly needed so that garages, then so called, sold cars and repaired them as well as supplying petrol to customers in the town.

Top: Horse-drawn waggons heading northwards to the quay (Tuck)

Bottom left: Polka Road (New Road) in the early years of the 20th century with young horse chestnut trees on the left hand side (Comma)

Bottom right: The same view in 2021 (Gower)

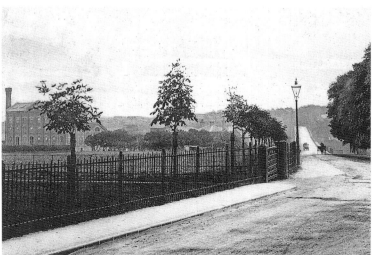

Top left: Rose's Garage on Polka Road in the 1920s

Top right: Garage on Polka Road, for many years owned by George Cain and then by Stacey Walsingham (Tuck)

Bottom left: Rose's Court, site of the former garage, in 2021 (Gower)

Bottom right: Self service station with Cooperative store adjacent (Gower)

Arguably the earliest garage which sold petrol to the public was Rose's garage on Polka Road. Rose had an ironmongers on High Street. George Turner Cain opened his garage further down a year or so later in 1924. Sam Abel's garage was on the quay. There was another at the end of Burnt Street. More would come. Having had half a dozen petrol stations at one time, the town had, for a long time, none at all until a self-service petrol station was built on Polka Road in 2018.

Top left: Regal Cinema in the 1960s (Tuck)

Top right: Closed in 1974, it was converted into flats in 1981 (Gower)

Clubbs Lane

Newgates Lane in 1970 with the cinema auditorium to the right (Shackle)

Below centre: Oddfellows Court on Newgates Lane 2020 (Arguile)

Below right: Demolition in 1981 (Tipler)

Clubbs Lane, just round the corner from Staithe Street, was never a major thoroughfare but its contribution to Wells life needs a mention. Apart from its rather grand Scarborough Hotel, originally built as a manse, (and subsequently as an old people's home) it was where the Regal cinema was located. Live entertainment in the form of a theatre had existed in the nineteenth century (see page 68). The theatre is long gone though the building survived until the 1960s when the whole area was felled. 'Canned' entertainment came to Wells in 1914 as an occasional feature, and became regular in 1929 when the Oddfellows Hall on Clubbs Lane was first hired out and, in 1937 was converted into a permanent cinema. A huge shed with a steel frame and concrete blocks was built behind it as the auditorium extending to Newgates Lane.

It showed feature films, often more than a year after release but remained popular until television eventually killed it. It had served locals, visitors and servicemen and women before and during the war. Children's matinees were a great draw in the 1950s. It attempted to remain profitable by showing X rated films in the 1970s, to a strictly adult audience. After closure it remained empty for some years until a local builder knocked the auditorium down and built a series of flats, known as Oddfellows Court in memory of its origins.

Top left: Tinker's Corner looking west before the post office was built (Tuck)

Top right: Staff of the post office in 1905 (Tuck)

Bottom left: London Provincial Bank on Station Road around 1900

Bottom right: The same view in 2021 opposite the (closed) Barclays Bank (Gower

Station Road

Station Road runs along the top of the ridge between Staithe Street and High Street. It still sports one public house and once had three (see page 84). It once had several banks; it now has only a post office. It had a Methodist chapel, now the library (see page 90).

In 1855 the East of England bank opened next door to what is now Jagger's pharmacy on Staithe Street; it would change its name successively before moving to Station Road as the London Provincial bank. Seen lower left it was until recently an opticians.

The post office was once on High Street but in 1905 the current Post Office was built.

The branch of Barclays which closed in 2019 had opened in 1884 as a branch of the Fakenham Bank and then rapidly as Gurneys, Birbeck, Barclay and Buxton bank. It became Barclays in 1897. In 1922 it absorbed the London Provincial bank and the building was completely demolished and rebuilt in 1963.

The Yards

The former Sun Yard with the quay beyond (Tuck)

The former Sun Yard with entry to the yard seen from the quay 2020 (Gower)

Jicklings Yard looking out to sea (Shackle)

The many yards that run down to the quay and to Freeman Street from Theatre Road are all of them narrow but all of them different. Dating back several hundred years, they are recorded in the 1813 Enclosure document which identified every piece of property in the town, mostly named. Even before that, the yards give evidence of the huge prosperity of the town in the eighteenth century when Wells outstripped every port save Yarmouth, as already described (see page 2).

Some of the merchants' houses can be seen, standing above the quay. Thus while some yards have the names of the public houses at their foot, others give evidence of the merchants who lived there.

Sun Yard once ran down the side of the complex of maltings that became part of the Eastern Counties Farmers Cooperative (see pages 26–27). It was named after a public house, long gone. The yard was lost during the 1960s due to the initiative of the owner of the building to its east. With government collusion, it became part of Platten's fish shop. It was contended that the adjacent Jicklings Yard, which still remains, provided adequate access to the quay. The property was the former Sun Inn (see page 87) as the name implies.

Jicklings Yard, which still exists, was named after a sail maker, Francis Jickling, who moved to Wells from Brancaster sometime around the 1780s and who at one time owned a rope walk on the Buttlands. Sail making had been one of the unsung trades of the town for several generations, an adjunct to the growing ship building industry in Wells. Jickling had learned his trade in King's Lynn and employed a number of apprentices in the town.

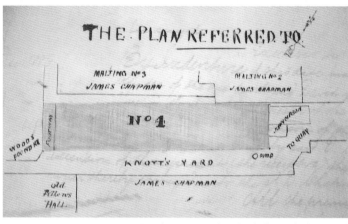

Top left: Green's Fish and Chip shop on Red Lion Yard

Top right: Red Lion Yard running down the east side of the Memorial Club (Shackle)

Centre left: Tunns Yard during new house building in the 1980s (Tipler)

Centre right: 19th century sketch plan of the maltings on Knotts Yard

Bottom: Knotts Yard looking south in 2020 (Arguile)

Red Lion Yard, which latterly boasted one of Wells' several fish and chip shops, also gave access to several large houses. Its crooked roadway has a house with a flying freehold, one of two remaining in the town, as well as several corn storage properties. To the west Tunns Yard, by comparison, is straight, running down by the side of the Pauls' huge maltings (see pages 29-30). Its demolition and rebuilding in 1984 left the front of the No. 18 building behind which was built a row of houses which back onto Knotts Yard. Now unnamed because no houses front onto it, it remains unmetalled as did all the yards a hundred years ago.

On the west side of the Glebe lay a

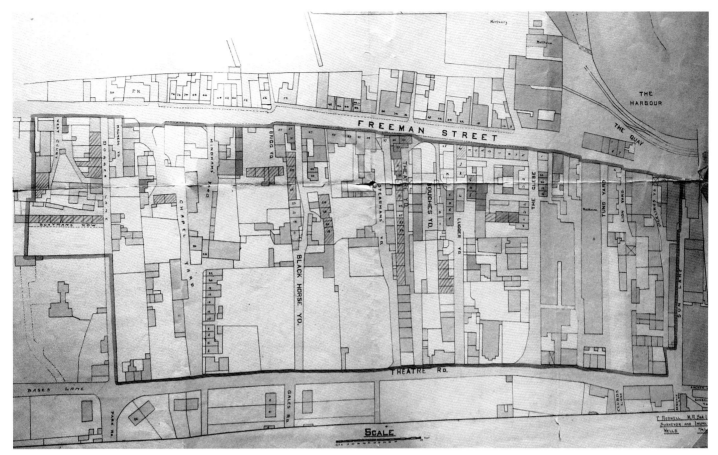

The yards to the west of the Glebe were the subject of a proposed Improvement Area in 1933 which was implemented in part after the Second World War. The map above shows the names of the many yards, some of which completely disappeared in the 1960s. Not all are named

number of yards only one of which survives at all. Lugger Yard is but a stub of itself leading to a car park. It was for many years a wasteland following pre-war demolition. Before that it had been a hive of life, but many of its people poor, its houses hard to keep clean.

Stearmans Yard which ran parallel to it survives only as a the name of the car park. Rackhams Yard, Theatre Yard and Bouches Yard remain on old maps and in some people's memories including Gibbs Yard and Playhouse Yard.

The intended designation of the yards as an Improvement Area in 1933 was hindered by the war and a smaller area than originally planned was finally de-

Lugger Yard following a pre-war demolition (Tuck)

The Busby and Gee families pose for a picture in Glebe Yard, pre-WWI (Tuck)

Stearman's Yard – long gone (Tuck)

molished in 1962. Proposals to build sixty-seven houses, four flats and sixty-five garages and a major road to take harbour traffic out of town came to nothing.

The fate of the yards where the car park now stands could have befallen those further west. By the 1970s they were many of them not in a good state. Demolished cottages were left to grow weeds or used as parking spaces.

Blackhorse Yard was in a parlous state. The signs of former occupation were all too visible where ranges and fire-places were all that was left of former houses, cleared as being insanitary or incapable of economic repair. Caravans were stored among the houses because the Pinewoods caravan park at the north end of the Beach Road did not permit caravans to remain on site during the winter months. It was a minor source of income for local people to store them in their yards during the period. As caravans became larger this arrangement proved impossible to continue.

Eventually, it would be private initiative which would improve the yards either by new building or by improving existing cottages. The Black Horse public house, seen on the opposite page beyond the nose of the parked car, is the only remaining building on that side of the yard to remain. The others have been replaced.

Chapel Yard, further west, was much wider and gives all the appearance of having scarcely changed, except of course, that even with the enlargement of some cottages and knocking two into one of others, they were not really suitable for bringing up young families. The cottages would become dark in winter as they were bought as holiday homes.

Theatre Road itself was named after

Top left: Signs of former occupation – a range downstairs and a fireplace upstairs (Shackle)

Top right: Blackhorse Yard car parking (Shackle)

Bottom left: Blackhorse Yard with parked caravans in 1970 (Shackle)

Bottom right: Blackhorse Yard in 2020 (Gower)

Left: Dogger Lane in 1970 (Shackle)

Top right: Chapel Yard in 1970 (Shackle)

Middle right: Fisher's Theatre converted to housing, before being demolished (Tuck)

Bottom right: Magness Yard in 1970 (Shackle)

the Fisher theatre, built in 1812 and closed in 1844. It was converted into housing and was finally demolished in 1965. Magness Yard, a blind yard between Chapel Yard and Dogger Lane, completely disappeared with new buildings. Dogger Lane survived relatively intact.

New Housing

Wells was well ahead of most places in the country in its council housing programme. Remarkably begun during the First World War following pressure from Sam Peel, newly elected in 1913, the Earl of Leicester made the land available and officiated at the dedication of the plaque on Northfield Lane in 1915. There followed a row of houses on Mill Road (then called Park Road) running westwards out of town. Gales Road followed in 1924 before the expansion of the Northfield Estate and Westfield Avenue at the other end of the town.

Various plans were made during the 1930s resulting in the building of more houses on Northfield. Some plans were delayed by the war but by 1951 over 350 such houses had been built, thus rehousing local families from the cramped and often insanitary yards running down to the quay.

Above left: Laying the memorial plaque 1915 (Tuck)

Left: Mill Road house building in 1921 (French)

Centre: Mill Road houses in 1991 (Tipler)

Right: Northfield Waye estate in the 1950s (Facebook)

Historic Houses

The White House on Burnt Street in 1970 (Shackle)

The Well House on Standard Road, built circa 1680 (Shackle)

Brigg Square, a close of houses dated to 1648 (Shackle)

Wells is not notable for its great houses. The aristocracy lived in Holkham and Walsingham. There were, however, a number of merchants' houses, some of which have survived externally almost unchanged. A small number are known to date from the seventeenth century. The White House, a double gabled building on Burnt Street to the south of the town, is one such.

Another, almost on the quay, is the Well House created from a row of cottages, probably in the 1600s. It is recorded as being sold in 1725 for £150, a substantial sum even to the Wells merchant, Henry Woodrow. Its ownership by mariners and shipwrights makes sense from its position and its high viewing window which enabled those who lived there to see when a ship was coming in. High dormer windows were common.

Wells had for a long time traded in coal and grain. The big growth in its mercantile activities was during the eighteenth century when the overseas trade in malt with the continent was at its height, as already described. Records exist of a substantial coal trade with the north east of England in the early 16th century. By the seventeenth century Wells' trade included such valuable commodities as saffron. Prosperity brought more house-building.

From the same century is a small close of houses on the south side of Freeman Street, known as Brig Square, whose dating is set out on its front wall – 1648.

Not all of the great houses face the sea. Ostrich House stands behind a stone wall in Burnt Street, just a stone's throw from the church. Dated to 1722, a new facade was added early in the following century. In 1822 it became an inn which it continued to be until the beginning of the Great War.

Above: Ostrich House on Burnt Street, sometime public house and private residence (Tuck)

Below left : Newgates House, off Newgates Lane, at one time another public house (Arguile)

Below right:: Two front doors, Nos 33 and 35 Staithe Street, behind a common entrance to Newgates House (Arguile)

Newgate House, now concealed behind shops on Staithe Street, was the sixteenth century abode of William Newgate, a considerable landowner with holdings in Holkham. It had a brewery, malthouses and other associated buildings. We know that he bequeathed it to his widow in 1667. By the eighteenth century it was leased by the banking family of Peckover after which it became the Three Swans public house and subsequently the Duke's Head. In the 1820s three shops were built in front of it and it was divided into two properties. The set-back entrances can be seen between two shops today.

Mayshiel, on the east side of Staithe Street, merits its own entry. Built orig-

inally in 1740, it stands on what was once the extensive property of Elgar's House, now incorporated into several of the shops on Staithe Street. Perched on the brow of the hill, it has a lookout seawards. Its many windows, now blocked up, suggest that it did not face a street at all when built.

When the Smiths, not sea merchants but maltsters, acquired it in 1878 they spent over £1000 on alterations, probably blocking up windows and turning its aspect south. They renamed it after a shooting lodge in Scotland which they made use of. The huge garden was

Top left: Mayshiel in 1970 when it was still a private residence (Shackle)

Top right: Aerial view of Mayshiel garden (Cracknell)

Bottom left: The garden of Mayshiel in the 1920s (Tuck)

Bottom right: Once a pet store with flats and a coffee shop (Gower)

flanked to the west by a high wall behind which was a line of ilex trees. They opened it to the public for fetes and tennis matches.

The death of its owner, Edgar Ladas Smith, in 1929 put an end to such things but it wasn't developed until the 1970s. The house was for a long time a pet store and a number of coffee shops, with flats above.

The Normans, on Standard Road, was developed on the site of several cottages in 1793 by John Bloom. He was one of a family of seafarers and later ship owners and merchants of the town probably going back to the early seventeenth century.

Bloom fell on hard times financially and in 1833 the house was sold to the first of a succession of doctors in the town, all confusingly named Hugh Rump. It subsequently passed to several

Above: South facing to catch the sun, The Normans is an example of late Georgian building (Shackle)

Below left: The Normans, now part of a close of houses, 2021 (Arguile)

Below centre: Entrance in 1970 (Shackle)

Below right: The Normans' stables, long disused, in 1970 (Shackle)

Top: Bishop Ingle House in 1970 (Shackle)

Bottom left: Bishop Ingle House in its clergy holiday home days (Tipler)

Bottom centre: Marsh House on Marsh Lane (Tipler)

Bottom right: Marsh House in the course of renovation 2021 (Arguile)

generations of doctors and medical officers of health ending with the retirement of Dr 'Willie' Hicks in 1969. The loss of the surgery was one of the reasons for the building of the Health Centre only a couple of hundred yards away.

The Normans' garden was then made into Invaders' Court, a close of houses all named after invaders.

The Lawn, now Bishop Ingle House, on Clubbs Lane was for a long time the house of one of the two solicitors' families in the town, EB Loynes and Sons. For a short while it was known as Bank House because it was the location of the earliest banking facilities in the town. Previously, the Gales family ran an adjoining plant nursery, but the house dates back to the eighteenth century and was for a long time owned by the absentee Girdlestone family. Post-war it was made into a clergy holiday home named after the son of a onetime vicar of the parish who became a suffragan bishop. It is now in private hands again.

Marsh House, built in 1742, lies on the north side of Church Marsh. It was variously occupied by Hugh Rump, already mentioned, and much later by another surgeon, Alfred Whitlock, who

was also registrar of births, marriage and deaths. It was bought by George Smith the maltster and later still by George Turner Cain, a controversial town councillor and garage owner. It has recently been the object of substantial renovation to restore it to its former glory.

Blenheim House at the western end of the town overlooking the west marsh comes from the same period. The first of the Rumps moved there in 1811. It was briefly a boarding school in the 1860s and was later the residence of one of the Loynes family.

Some buildings defy attempts to identify their origins. One such is on Star Yard behind Staithe Street, a huge house dating back again to the seventeenth century but possibly earlier but without any clue as to its date or significance. Others like Elgars House are not easily recognisable; part of it is a shop on Staithe Street. A row of outbuildings now forms Elgars Row which backs onto Shop Lane.

Among the many concealed buildings stands Westward House, originally Westward Ho! which is set back from Mill Road just beyond the Buttlands. Among its many owners was Peter Hudson, a prominent miller of the town who owned several of the windmills which

Above: The 'Manor House' on Star Yard 2020 (Arguile)

Below left: Westward Ho! may date back to the sixteenth century when it would have been a farmhouse (Tipler)

Below right: Blenheim House on Theatre Road

stood along the ridge which runs westward out of the town.

The renovation and updating of ancient houses is a sensitive matter. It has also meant the saving of several buildings which were in danger of being lost. Clarence House, built as part of the mercantile development of the nineteenth century and at one time in the ownership of the Dalliston family, was left empty for thirty or more years and was in danger of being lost. The roof was at the point of falling in. Its restoration has included the removal of later additions and the rebuilding of the rear.

The oldest part of Croft House dates from the seventeenth century. The later additions to the west and the new facade appear to be 18th century, possibly added by Thomas Bolton, a grain and coal merchant, who was married to Susannah Nelson, the sister of Lord Admiral Horatio Nelson. Lord Nelson is known to have visited the house in Wells with Lady Hamilton during his time ashore between 1787 and 1793. The house was subsequently occupied by the foreman of the Granary, Thomas Batterby, until the closure of the maltings in 1929. It became a tenement house for up to four families, until being sold to the Scoles family in the 1950s. It has been modernised and extended since 2019.

The Buttlands

The Buttlands from the north showing the bandstand, pre WWI (Tuck)

The Square House, built in 1825 (Shackle)

Monteagle on the east side of The Buttlands, 1970 (Shackle)

Sometimes suggested as former archery butts, the Buttlands was more probably just a piece of land abutting the town. In the 1820s it became a fashionable place for the gentry to live, its westward side being developed at the end of the Georgian period.

The ownership of the Buttlands was long disputed between Wells Urban District Council and the Holkham Estate. Both claimed title and therefore the rent from events such as a fair or market. After sharp correspondence in 1905 the estate agreed to a peppercorn rent paid by the council for a period after which they would assume the title. The deeds were handed over to the council in 1937.

The Square House was one of the first to be built in about 1825 and was bought by the first of a line of surgeons, the ubiquitous Rumps, who had just moved from Blenheim House (previous pages). By the 1860s the Buttlands had become the favoured address of solicitors, doctors, merchants, maltsters, shop-keepers, ship-owners and of two hotels, the Crown and the Globe (see page 83).

In 1903 a bandstand was built which survived until 1943 being used frequently in the early days by the town's brass band. Monteagle, now flats, was, along with Clarence House, among the favoured shooting hotels advertising itself as the Buttlands Hotel. The look of the Buttlands has not changed much over the years, but it is no longer the preferred place of residence of the business people of the town.

The annual November bonfire celebrated by the town every year became a victim of the 2020 lockdown and increasing insurance problems and ceased that year, apparently never to return.

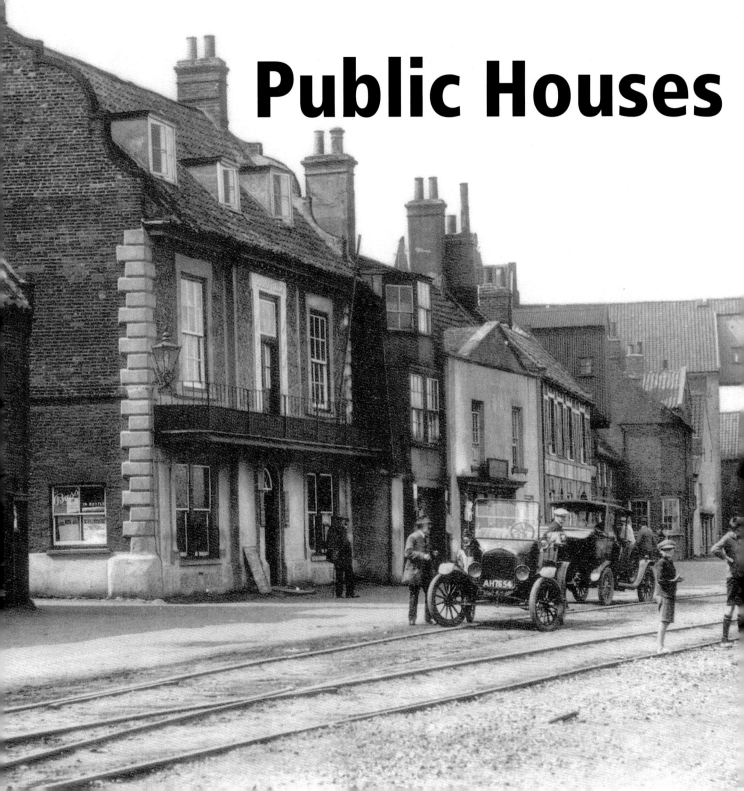

Public Houses

The Bowling Green at the turn of the 20th century (Tuck)

The Golden Fleece with a Model T Ford in the early part of last century (McCallum)

The Bowling Green in 1970 (Shackle)

Wells once had over fifty licensed premises though the highest number at any one time was thirty-two. The tightening of licensing regulations around the turn of the twentieth century resulted in a drastic reduction in the number of outlets to sixteen. Further reductions would take place down to the five now functioning. Many of the former public house buildings still remain.

Of those still in business among the oldest is the Bowling Green opposite the church which dates back at least to 1673. It has been almost continuously in operation since then, closing briefly in the 1990s. The Golden Fleece is certainly ancient. Parts of the building date from Tudor times The plaster reliefs of St. Blaise and of the Viking invasions have been dated to 1710. It was at one time the centre of the town's civic activities: the magistrates' court and the harbour authorities both met there until the Crown opened in 1830. Stage coaches left from there until about the same time.

The two establishments on the Buttlands, the Crown, built in 1830 and the Globe about the same vintage remain in business.

The Crown's first landlord Samuel Ellis had transferred from the Ostrich (see page 73) to take advantage of the growing importance of the Buttlands as a centre of the town's civic and commercial activity, having previously owned the Royal Standard on the quay. It became the place for town meetings, the magistrates' court and the departure point for stage coaches. It was the preferred place for the gentry to stay. It encouraged cyclists.

The Globe's adjacent Assembly Rooms provided theatrical entertainment for the town in the late nineteenth

The Crown in the 1920s (Tuck)

The Cyclists' Touring Club logo above the main entrance of The Crown (Tuck)

The Globe was run for many years by the Cawdron family (Tuck)

century after which it fell on hard times and was bought by Herbert Cawdron, whose family ran it for many years. It was for a short time owned by the Holkham Estate and is now an independent operation, having converted its former Assembly Rooms into bed and breakfast accommodation.

The Edinburgh at the top of High Street was previously the Leicester Arms (and before that the Fighting Cocks) and was renamed and rebuilt in 1887 by James Alexander Davidson who also owned the Fleece and the Crown. He was a coal merchant, a wine and spirit merchant and a cartridge manufacturer. As the Fighting Cocks it dates back to the eighteenth century and may be older.

At the east end of Station Street the variously named Railway and Tinkers Hotel, latterly the Lifeboat was built in 1845 to catch the anticipated railway traffic.

Above left: The Edinburgh in the 1970s since when the interior has been much remodelled and the exterior painted (Shackle)

Above right: The Railway Hotel at the turn of the 20th century (Warren)

Right: The Railway Hotel, renamed the Lifeboat Inn with its sun room bricked in and a sloping roof added. It has since been repainted dark grey (Hissey)

The Shipwrights was a fisherman's pub (Warren)

The Shipwrights bar in the 1970s (Comma)

The Ship Inn transferred its licence to the newly built Ark Royal in 1967 (Shackle)

The Ark Royal ended its days in 2020 (Hissey)

By the time it was taken over by Watneys in 1967, the railway had closed so that it was renamed the Tinkers Hotel. Becoming the Lifeboat in 1994 it closed in 2020.

Of the many east end pubs of yesteryear the Shipwrights was the last survivor, its name testifying to the existence of two shipyards at the east end. The Jolly Sailors had closed in 1884, the Norfolk Freeholders in 1905. It was a fisherman's pub, standing opposite the fishermen's cooperative. The grounds outside, the so-called drying grounds, were widely used by families wishing to take advantage of both what it had to provide, and the view. The upstairs room was at one time used by the Hydroplane Club for their meetings. It closed in the 1980s.

The Ship, at the opposite end of the quay on Freeman Street, was also a local haunt. It closed in 1967 when the brewery, Bullards, had the licence transferred to the Ark Royal. In its new home it became a popular pub for discos. However, after a number of attempts to rebrand it, first as the Captain's Table and then as Harleys, (in which incarna-

The Shipwrights was a
The Royal Standard, one
of the oldest pubs in the
town, in 1910 (Comma)

Standard House in 1970 when
it was an antique shop
(Shackle)

tion it never actually opened), it was
demolished in 2020.

The huge number of buildings which
were once licensed as public houses, inns
or taverns are too many to record here.
Some of them though need a mention.
The Royal Standard, until recently a
chandlery, closed in 1905 as the authorities sought to reduce the number of
licensed premises in the town. Dating
back at least until the eighteenth century, Parson Woodforde stayed there in
1779. It was the place for public meetings, auctions of ships and the cargoes
of wrecks, and was an early departure
point for stage coaches circa 1780.

The Prince of Wales, previously the
Tewkesbury Arms, can be dated to 1868
taking the later name from a pub of that
name in High Street which had closed.
It closed in 1966 and is now a café.

The variously named Six Ringers and
Eight Ringers was on Church Plain.
Like so many houses in Wells it was
taken on by Bullards who sold out to
Watneys in the 1960s. They closed it in
1971.

Along the quay there were at least
eight public houses, many of which have

The Eight Ringers in the
1950s (Tuck)

The Prince of Wales in 1979
(Shackle)

The Lord Nelson (centre) which was replaced by amusements (Tuck)

The former Sun Inn, now a fish and chip shop, was a coffee shop in the 1970s (Comma)

The Vine on High Street (Comma)

The Vine ceased trading in 1985 and is now Angus House, a private residence (Shackle)

left no trace. Of the Brewers Arms, there is scarcely a photograph. Of the Lord Nelson, there are pictures: it lay approximately where Grays amusements were until the fire of 2005 and which is now a block of flats.

The Sun Inn whose licence was not renewed in 1925, is now a restaurant and fish and chip shop, having been a tea room for a while.

The Queen Adelaide on Freeman Street was popular with service personnel during WWII. It closed in 1951.

On High Street, none of the pubs remain though some of the buildings are still extant. The Duke's Head on the west side of the road was a new building around 1870 on the site of the Green Dragon which goes back at least to 1789 and was closed in 1865. The Vine, a Morgan's pub, was taken over first by Steward and Patterson's and then by Watneys who closed it in 1967.

The Churches

There has been a church on the site of the current St Nicholas' church at the junction of Church Street and Church Plain probably since the conquest but the first church of which we have a picture was built about 1460. The building which we now see, however, was rebuilt in 1883 after a fire in 1879 which destroyed everything but the tower. Even that had to be substantially repaired in 1967 and again in 2023.

Church choirs, consisting largely of local boys, are now a thing of the past. For that reason the chancel stalls where they sat have been removed and an altar placed at its west end facing the people.

Methodists have been strong in Norfolk since their creation in the eighteenth century. They had started off meeting in people's cottages, breaking into two and then several more branches. The Wesleyan Methodist church on Station Road opened in 1808; the Primitive Methodist chapel on Theatre Road opened in 1891.

The two branches came together in

Top left: The church before the fire of 1879 (Tuck)

Top right: After the fire, 1879 (Tuck)

Centre left: Tower repairs in 1967

Centre right: St Nicholas church choir in 1929 (Tuck)

Bottom: Interior of the rebuilt church (Tuck)

The Primitive Methodist church on Theatre Road

The Wesleyan Methodist chapel in 1920 (Comma)

The Methodist church on Theatre Road (Shackle)

The chapel was converted into the town library (Shackle)

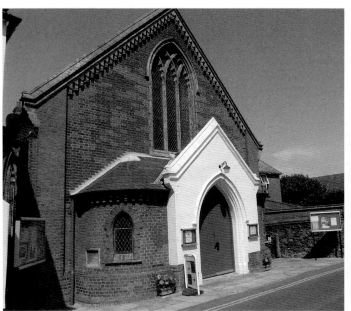

The Quaker Meeting House in 1970 (Comma)

Wells Congregational church (Shackle)

1932 which resulted in the decision to close one of the two chapels in Wells. It was the Station Street Wesleyan chapel which was closed. It was bought by the Urban District Council in 1936 for use as the town's library. It opened finally in 1949.

The Theatre Road chapel became the Methodist church of the town.

The Friends' Meeting House, on Church Street, dates back in origin to 1680, making it the oldest dissenting body in the town. It was enlarged in the early nineteenth century, later taking in part of the Wells workhouse site for its burial ground. After a period of decline it revived in the last century due to the efforts of local councillor, Sam Peel.

The Congregational church on Clubbs Lane was built in 1817 and enlarged in 1826. Scarborough House, now a care home, further down the Lane was built as a manse and Sunday school for the church.

The first Roman Catholic church was the last to be built. The first such church since the Reformation was built in 1928 on the Buttlands. Opened with great ceremony, it was initially the subject of vandalism and graffiti. Good relations between churches now result in joint effort and occasional joint services.

The consecration of the Catholic church in 1928 (Tuck)

Consecration service 1928 (Tuck)

Floods

After the 1897 flood

West Marsh looking towards Freeman Street)Tuck)

The backs of houses on Freeman Street (Tuck)

Wells has been subject to flooding from high tides over centuries. Those of 1897 left a vessel on the roadway at the east end.

The flood of 1953 was, however, the most devastating. The beach bank was breached in three places; houses on Freeman Street were awash, some had lost their outside walls; hundreds of farm animals were drowned, their bloated bodies lying on the marsh for days afterwards. The Pinewoods camp with its café was devastated. Over 300 people died along the coast though none in Wells. It was nine months before the breaches were finally filled and some kind of normality was restored to the town. Over £16,000 was raised for the town to relieve the losses sustained by householders and shopkeepers

1953

Below right: The remains of Pinewoods campsite with the lifeboat station in the distance

Beach Bank breached
near Pinewoods (Comma)

Apart from the beach bank, north point bank was overtopped flooding the railway and the south end of the town. The bank at Burnham Overy also went bringing more water to the west marshes and tearing the Heacham line railway track from its bed. Vessels were lifted onto the quay, including the former air sea rescue boat the *Terra Nova* owned by the Sea scouts.

Far right: Railway line to
Heacham washed away
(Tuck)

Right: vessel *Terra Nova*
washed up onto the quay
(Tuck)

Above: Beach huts after the surge (Tuck)

Top right: Sailing cruisers on the quay (Tuck)

Centre right: Trinity pilot boat smashed on the quay (Tuck)

Bottom right: The five hundred ton coaster *Function* on the quay (Tuck)

1978

The 1978 flood was just as severe as the earlier one though it produced much less damage. The beach bank was again breached but the houses were less severely damaged and the repairs were executed much more quickly. Leisure boats, which were much fewer in 1953, were lifted up and dumped on the quay together with a coaster, the *Function*, whose removal presented a much bigger problem. A fishing boat, the *Strandline* was carried through a breach, coming to rest on the fields beyond as the tide receded.

Helicopters were brought in to fill the breaches in the bank with material from the lime works but without much success; each tide was liable to wash away the work. It was the arrival of Dutch engineers with their pumping equip-

ment who were able to fill the breach so that this time the caravan site was able to open by the Whitsun (Spring) bank holiday, though it all looked pretty bleak.

It was clearly essential that the Beach Bank be raised and the harbour improved. A moveable barrier across the west end of the quay was built in 1982 which saved the houses on Freeman Street when another tidal surge took place in 2013. By then the wooden top to the retaining wall had been replaced by glass which held well. Nevertheless, Standard House was chest deep in water.

Top: Heavy machinery working on the beach bank

Centre left: Helicopter delivering lime from local works (Comma)

Centre right: Piles to strengthen the harbour wall in 1982 (Tuck)

Bottom: Moveable barrier in place which saved the west end from inundation in 2013 (Tuck)

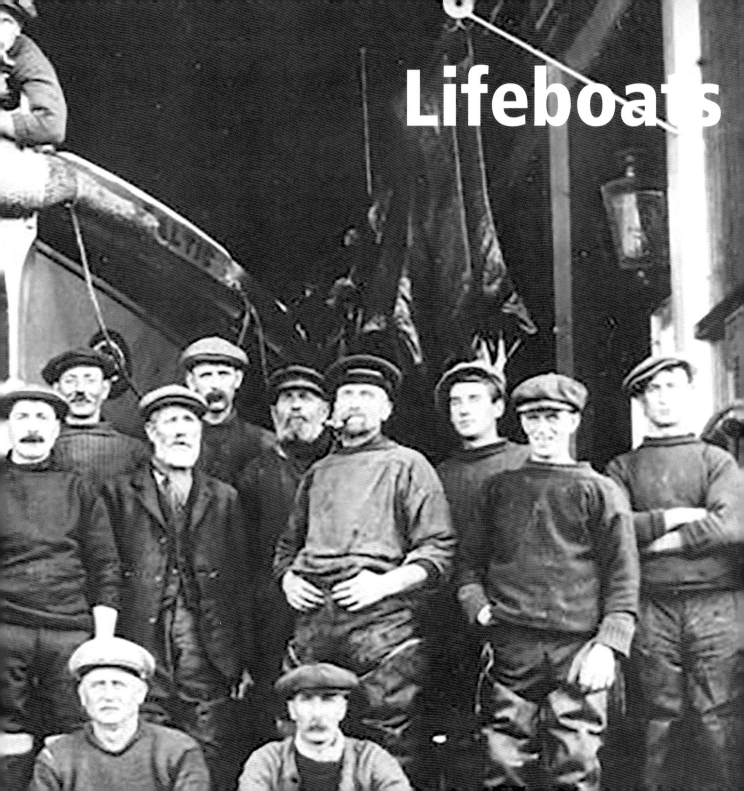
Lifeboats

Eliza Adams about to be launched (Tuck)

Lifeboat *Plymouth* in sail in Wells harbour (Tuck)

Dedication of *Baltic No 3* in 1919 (Tuck)

The importance of having some means of saving men from shipwreck was recognised as early as 1830 and the obligation to provide a vessel was contained in local legislation in 1844. Before then, and even later there were those who saw vessels that had run aground as providing an opportunity for salvage. What was also needed was a purpose-built lifeboat and a station in which to house it. These came about in 1869 when the *Eliza Adams* came on station. Costing £500 she was named after the wife of a Suffolk surgeon who had collected the necessary funds. She was propelled by twelve oarsmen. She proved her worth time and again and was famously lost attempting to save the crew of a third vessel that day, the *Ocean Queen* on the night of 29 October 1880.

Sails were an additional as a means of propulsion even well into the twentieth century when successive boats were supported by the Baltic Exchange, a London-based maritime trading market, and hence named *Baltic*.

The first powered lifeboat, the *Royal Silver Jubilee,* came on station in 1936. The crew was entirely composed of fishermen, including the coxswain Ted Neilsen, who had settled in Wells from his native Denmark. Horses had been replaced by a crawler tractor which could take the boat over the sands and out to sea at low tide. The *Jubilee* saw out the war to be replaced by a twin-screw boat, the *Cecil Paine*, in 1945 which was in turn followed by the *Ernest Tom Nethercoat* in 1965. By this time, skippered by David Cox, the second of his family to be coxswain, the *Ernest Tom* was engaged in the nearly fatal *Savinesti* incident when they stood by a Romanian coaster in hurricane force winds. The relief boat, *Lucy Lavers*, which had

Ted Neilsen (with cap, third from right) and crew of the *Royal Silver Jubilee* (Tuck)

Ernest Tom Nethercoat and *Doris M Mann of Ampthill* side by side in 1990 (Golding)

The *Duke of Edinburgh* arrives in Wells, 2022 (Arguile)

seen service at Dunkirk (and which is now in Wells harbour) saw service during those years.

In 1990 the *Doris M Mann of Ampthill* came on station. She was destined to become the longest serving lifeboat in the fleet, remaining on duty until 2023. A Mersey class all-weather lifeboat, she was the first to have a fully enclosed cockpit. The next generation represented an entirely new technology, a Shannon class all weather boat. Capable of over 30 knots, the crew of the *Duke of Edinburgh*, which arrived in 2022, have the use of very high-tech navigational and other aids as well as seating designed to allow travel at high speeds without unacceptable levels of discomfort, giving her the means of reaching vessels far out to sea in a very short time. The more regular call-outs, to pick up walkers caught out by the incoming tides, were dealt with by the new breed of inshore inflatable lifeboats.

The first lifeboat station, now the harbour office, was built in 1869. Being some distance from the sea, at low tide a lifeboat would be hauled to deep water on its carriage by horses and, at high tide, towed out to sea by the steam tugs then operating in the harbour.

A new lifeboat station was built on the beach in 1895, thus enabling lifeboats to proceed to sea immediately when the tide was in. When the tide was out, as now, the boat had to be taken across the sand, something that in the early days was achieved by a team of horses.

The old station was then sold to the town council who let it out as the Jubilee tea rooms. Named as a commemoration of Queen Victoria's diamond jubilee in 1897, it remained in use for many years until becoming the harbour

office. The new station was modified at different times as boats became larger. When motorised semi-submersible tractors were introduced to take the lifeboat over the sands at low tide and to retrieve and re-house it, it became necessary to have a southern slipway and entrance.

In 1990 it was extended further and re-roofed to accommodate the *Doris Mann*, to house an inshore inflatable boat and to create a crew room on the first floor. It was finally taken down in 2022 when the current, much larger station was built on higher ground, adjacent to the beach bank, to accommodate the *Duke of Edinburgh*, and to provide a visitor engagement area and souvenir shop with easy public access.

Top left: First lifeboat station, built in 1869, before conversion to the Jubilee tea rooms

Top right: Second station, as originally built in 1895 (Marshall)

Centre left: Second station modified to allow for larger boats (Tuck)

Centre right: Station re-roofed and extended in 1990 (RNLI)

Right: Current station completed in 2022 (RNLI)

Farming

Horse-drawn ploughs, little changed over hundreds of years (Temple)

Horse-drawn reaper binders bound the cut corn into sheaves

A dozen men haymaking at Wighton between the wars (Temple)

The revolution in farming in the last hundred years has been massive: from horse-drawn ploughs to tractors; from tractors to the huge variety of specialised machinery; from ploughing to cultivation on stubble without the use of a plough; but most of all, the disappearance of human beings from the fields. Until 1945 horse power and manpower, human muscle, would do almost everything. The fields were full of folk. At haysel – the hay harvest – and corn harvest dozens of Wells people would work in the fields. Until the war, horses pulled ploughs, seed drills, harrows, rollers, reaper binders and waggons; everything that had to be moved. A ploughman might walk eleven miles a day behind a plough horse. He would keep the plough in good repair and the horse in good health by his own efforts. Seed drills were horse drawn. A horse-drawn reaper binder would cut and bind the corn into sheaves which were gathered into stooks and taken to be threshed. Hand scythes were still used to clear the entrance to the field.

The harvesting of brassicas, sprouts, cabbages and cauliflowers would bring

Top left: Ploughing with traction engines on Branthill Farm, early 20th century (Tuck)

Top right: Post-WWII reaper binder tractor hauled on New Farm (Temple)

Above: Reaping with a combine harvester, New Farm 1980s (Temple)

Right: Crawler tractor ploughing on New Farm 1970s (Temple)

local people, mostly women, onto the fields to pick them.

Norfolk was essentially an agricultural county. It is not surprising therefore that the headquarters of the Agricultural Trade Union was in Fakenham, itself a small agricultural community at the turn of the twentieth century.

Mechanisation came in stages. The big development was the combustion engine, first steam-powered and then petrol and diesel engined. Traction engines were too heavy for ploughing except to haul a plough from one side of a field to another on a cable, an engine at each side. Tractors, which were imported from the 1920s, took over from horses only after the Second World War, first of all pulling machinery not much changed from earlier days. Many tasks, still performed by hand would soon be given over to machinery. The combine harvester allowed both reaping and threshing in one operation, the grain to be poured into a waiting trailer. Tractors bore more heavily on the soil than horses, for which reason crawler tractors, which distributed their weight more evenly, were one of a number of experiments intended to make the land more productive.

John Temple, who took over New Farm in 1950, became an exemplar of new methods, introducing different crops such as carrots which were washed after harvest and dispatched in bags. He experimented with chickens, at one time produced eggs in such quantity that he was able to sell them to Sainsburys. At one time he had six tractors and two combines, employing 30 men as late as 1975. Some old practices remained such as building and thatching a haystack, but they were soon to be superseded.

The milking of dairy cows required

Above: Temple's farm workers 1955 (Davey)

Below left: Three dairymaids on Flints Farm in the 1960s. Gladys Sampher is on the right (Vertigan)

Below right: Percy Phillips shearing sheep (Temple)

their being driven through the town twice a day. Hand milking continued until the War when milking machines dispensed with milkmaids and the task became one performed mostly by men. Manor Farm, whose tenant, Ernest Flint had won prizes for milk production, reduced and then gave up dairying shortly after his death in 1957.

Temple decided to go in for sheep, and when he realised how intensive it was especially during lambing he employed Percy Phillips, himself the son of a shepherd to run his flock. As recently as the 1980s he could be seen driving them up Standard Road from the west marshes. Lambing took place often while snow was on the ground in order to make the spring market using hay bales to shelter the ewes.

Once sheep would be driven from the railway station to the various farms or along the lanes by the hundred as they had been a little over a century ago. In 1916, George Wright of Mill Farm bought and sold over 7,800 animals, mostly sheep, which were driven to and from his farm to outlying farms, to markets, to and from the station, and to butchers – of which there were seven in Wells alone. Once Ernest Flint had had over 200 beasts driven twice a day down Church Street to be milked.

The animals have not entirely gone from the fields around the town but they are no longer driven through it.

Tractors became more sophisticated. Ploughing, once thought basic, would give way over time to machinery which would plant cover crops and cover them in one operation on land on which maize had only recently been harvested, all without ploughing. Manure, formerly ploughed in, would be composted and spread among the cover crops ready for

Feeding dairy cows at New Farm (Temple)

the new season. All of this would take place hidden in plain sight from those who live in the town, some of whose forebears had been among the hundreds of cowmen, shepherds, tractor drivers, carpenters, pea pickers, brussels pickers, lorry drivers, carrot lifters, some for a while, and some for the whole of their working lives.

Percy Phillips leading sheep up Standard Road, 1980s

The Beach

Top left: Abraham's Bosom, a boating lake behind the Pinewoods, opened by the Earl of Leicester in 1935 (Tuck)

Top right: Woolterton's Beach café drew visitors, some arriving by bicycle in the early years of the century (Tuck)

Middle left: Abel's coach running from the beach to the town (Walker)

Middle right: Tents offered the most straightforward changing facilities at the turn of the century (Tuck)

Right: Huts built on stilts to protect them from high tides could be hired and used when the weather turned wet (Tuck)

Just as Wells once depended on the sea and its ability to deal with coastal communities along the coast and across the North Sea, bringing in fish, then coal and then a variety of other commodities and exporting the produce of the fields, so it has come to depend more and more on tourism and the beach. Seaside holidays date back to the eighteenth century but they became a serious attraction between the two world wars and since.

The Pinewoods caravan park became a separate community, only partially dependant on the town. Charabancs, as the first buses were called, taxis, coaches and even later a miniature railway carried people to and from the town. Bicycles and then cars caused the expansion of the cark park. In 1935 the Earl of Leicester opened a boating lake.

Caravans came in increasing numbers. Some would remain all summer, presenting increasing problems to their owners and to Wells Council which would not allow them to remain all summer (many would be stored in unlikely places in the town (see page 67).

The day trippers came to the railway station and were brought to the beach by taxi or bus. Once on the beach they would be provided with what they needed: food and drink. Refreshments provided ranged from full meals to tea and coffee, buns and ice cream.

The beach itself provided opportunities for swimming and sunbathing. Changing facilities started with tents and proceeded to the building of beach huts which would eventually extend for over half a mile along the edge of the Pinewoods. The land on which they stood belonged to the estate but even leasehold they would come to cost more than the price of a house in the town fifty years earlier.

War and tidal surges would, in their

As far back as the first decade of the century, trips out to sea were being offered to visitors. Note the tug *Marie* with her twin funnels (Tuck)

Built in 1976 and rebuilt after the flood and at first driven by live steam, the Harbour railway took visitors to the beach until 2021 when it was replaced by a bus (Facebook)

different ways, put paid to them. During the Second World War access to the beach huts was banned and, if they were not taken down they would be confiscated, or they would fall prey to the elements. The tidal surges of 1953 and 1978 caused huge damage (see pages 93-96).

In good times other attractions would be the opportunity to take to the water on a boat, something that local fishermen would be quick to make provision for. These days people bring their own kayaks and paddle boards.

As always there are more pictures and more stories than can easily be contained in a book. What is set out here may however enable readers to understand how some of the features of Wells have come to be as they are and what we have lost. Change is constant and may even be increasing its pace.

Wells has ceased to look to the land or the land to look to the town. It has become a seaside resort full of holiday homes. Its attractions lie not only in its beach but also its character as a town which has retained visible reminders of its former self as a port, a fishery and an industrial base.

Now known for its shellfish, crabs, lobsters and whelks, its beach and its beach huts, its eating places, its quaint streets and traditional shops, that industrial and commercial past is quite unknown to many who come to visit or have bought second homes in the town. People often suggest that the town has not changed. In truth it has changed massively.

The evidences of its past make for the charm of the town but the story can be read more clearly if the former uses of present buildings are explained and the changes shown in pictures. That is what this book has been about.

Other books by Roger Arguile

A Church in a Landscape
A history of South Creake Church
(Jubilee 2011) 79pp
ISBN 978 0 9568515 0 5

A brief history of effects on the
life of a church, of changes in the
ecclesiastical outlook of the nation
and the response of the church at
large.

Other books by Roger Arguile

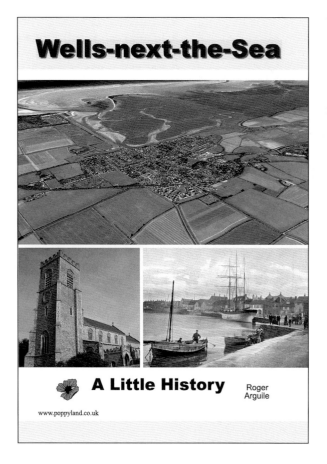

**Wells-next-the—Sea
A Little History
(Poppylands 2013) 36pp
ISBN 978 0 946148 99 8**

A brief introduction to
Wells-next-the-Sea, going back
to the Norman Conquest.

Other books by Roger Arguile

Wells–next–the–Sea
A small port and a wide world
(Poppylands 2014) 208 pp
ISBN 978 1 909796 49 2

Using original sources, this book is a longer account of the development of Wells-next-the-Sea from its early history, outlining its changing importance in the context of national events, religious and secular, landholding, the growth of industry particularly of malting, the importance of agriculture, shipping and ship building, fishing, the health and housing of its townspeople, war and the growth of tourism.

Other books by Roger Arguile

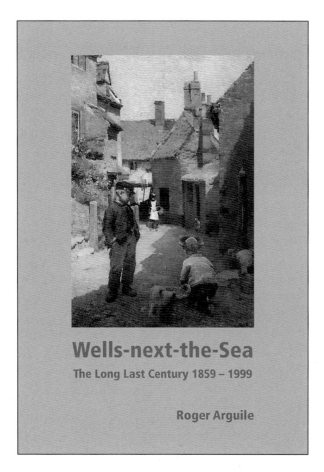

Wells-next-the-Sea
The Long Last Century
(Jubilee 2022) 265 pp
ISBN 978 0 9568515 12

Using sources such as school logbooks, minutes of the town's councils, hospital records and many conversations with local people, this book outlines a period of rapid change from the coming of the railway in 1857 to the end of the twentieth century.

It describes the decline of industry, the growth of educational provision, improvements in housing and public utilities, the changing fortunes of the port, fishing, war and flood, the town's social life and the human beings involved, some of whom were the architects of change, some of whom resisted change, and the accidental circumstance which made an industrial town into a tourist attraction